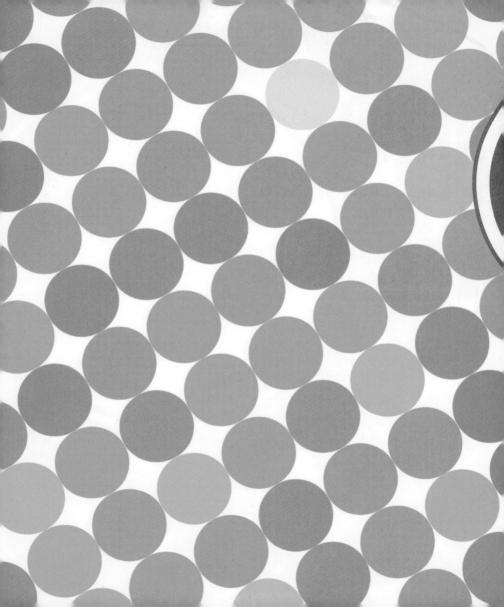

Women Ask
Women Answer

Questions Women Long to Ask,
Answers They Need to Know

Published by
THOMAS NELSON™
Since 1798

www.thomasnelson.com

TODAY'S CHRISTIAN
woman

Published in Nashville, Tennessee by Thomas Nelson. Thomas Nelson is a trademark of Thomas Nelson, Inc.

Thomas Nelson, Inc. titles may be purchased in bulk for educational, business, fundraising, or sales promotional use. For information, please e-mail SpecialMarkets@ThomasNelson.com.

Scripture quotations in this book are from *The New King James Version* (NKJV) ©1979, 1980, 1982, 1992, 2002 Thomas Nelson, Inc., Publisher; *The New International Version of the Bible* (NIV) © 1984 by the International Bible Society, used by permission of Zondervan Publishing House, all rights reserved; and *The New Living Translation* (NLT), © 1996, used by permission of Tyndale House Publishers, Inc., Wheaton, Illinois 60189. All rights reserved.

Project manager—Terri Gibbs

Designed by The Design Works Group, Sisters, Oregon.

ISBN
10: 1-4041-0452-6
13: 978-1-4041-0452-5

www.thomasnelson.com
www.christianitytoday.com

Printed and bound in China

Contents

Questions About . . .

Questions About

Friends

Q: I've recently moved. How do I make new friends?

A: Resist the urge to hibernate or you'll likely find yourself battling lone-liness. Instead, try the following friend-makers:

• *Ask someone for advice.* By putting the other person in the position of "expert," you make her less intimidated by the idea of getting to know you. Good questions include, "Where's a good place to go walking?" or "Who makes a dynamite cappuccino?" Before you know it, your expert might be offering to meet you at the little café that serves the best coffee in town.

• *Get involved in a church.* If you're a life-long Christian, this seems like a no-brainer. Yet, if you merely attend church services and Sunday school without getting involved, you'll likely find yourself a stranger even in a familiar place.

• *Join a group.* A great place to make friends is in a club or group of people with interests like yours. If you love to plant flowers, try a Master Gardener program; if you enjoy reading, join a book group.

• *Try something new.* The great thing about a move is being able to shake off everyone's expectations of who you are so you can start afresh. Always wanted to ski? Take some lessons. Thought about volunteering for Habitat for Humanity? Now's your opportunity. Chances are, you'll meet some potential friends along the way.

• *Make a memory.* A new friend and I decided to walk together for an hour once a week and to have breakfast once a month. That gives us a comfortable framework in which to explore a deeper relationship.

—Cindy Crosby, *Today's Christian Woman*, January/February 2002

Q: Should I maintain friendships with non-Christians? If so, how can I keep from compromising my faith?

A: As a woman in today's busy culture, you're often stretched to the limit. Friends sometimes are put on the back burner unless you see them as a regular part of your schedule.

If you're a Christian, most likely you spend the majority of your time with other Christians. That's good, because they keep you accountable and help you grow in the faith. You'll probably have to be intentional about friendships with non-believers; saying hello to the woman in the park who jogs there every Tuesday, inviting a new coworker out to lunch, knocking on a neighbor's door and offering fresh-baked cookies.

Jesus loved people, and so should you. But he also made clear that your top priority as a Christian is: to "love the Lord your God with all your heart, with all your soul, and with all your mind" (Matt. 22:37 NKJV). Thus, when you meet non-Christians, your goal should be not only to befriend them, but to introduce them to the Best Friend they could ever have—Jesus!

—*Christianity Today International*/Christian Bible Studies, 2001

FRIENDS

Q: How can I tell if a coworker is someone I will want to have as my friend?

A: Four questions might help you discern whether the woman you work with is someone you will want to befriend:

1. *How does she handle the truth?* Will she tell you when she thinks you're on the wrong path, or will she tell you only what she thinks you want to hear? How will she accept you if you tell her something she doesn't want to hear? A friend offers truth in a kind and loving package.

2. *Will she keep a private matter private?* Friendship grows through the intimate sharing of joys and sorrows that aren't for the whole world to know. Use restraint when sharing struggles with a new friend. Try her out on something small and see whether it makes its way back to you via the office grapevine.

3. *Is she secure enough not to get jealous?* It's hard to find anyone who doesn't carry with her some kind of personal agenda. Perhaps she tries to make herself look better by taking someone else down a rung or two. Perhaps she wants to befriend those who will help advance her career. Someone who is self-serving isn't trustworthy. Conversely, someone who has our best interests at heart is to be valued above all others.

4. *Will she challenge you to grow?* Friends sharpen, strengthen, and enhance our lives. As Ecclesiastes 4:9–10 says, "Two are better than one because they have a good return for their work: If one falls down, his friend can help him up. " (NIV)

—Julie-Alyson Ieron, *Today's Christian Woman*, May/June 2003

FRIENDS

Q: How can my husband and I find couples we both like to hang around with?

A: Making friends with other couples is a great way to discover more about your husband—and he about you—as you have fun with new people. Here are a few ideas to help you shape your search for couple friends.

• *Take a risk.* Don't be afraid to go outside your circle. Sometimes you can't tell from a surface acquaintanceship whether or not you'll hit it off with another couple. So don't be put off by such distinctions as, "Oh, but they have so much more money than we do," or "They seem more sophisticated than we are."

• *Go to church.* Get on a committee, participate in the mission conference or a kids' program, go to Sunday school, or join a Bible study. Work or study groups are great ways to meet people and connect with them on a regular basis.

• *Give it a good try.* There might be more misses than hits in your friendship adventures. Don't get discouraged. Enjoy each couple for their uniqueness. If a first visit with one couple seems awkward but hints at potential, make another date. The good news is that you never exhaust the supply of people around you.

• *Keep learning.* If you get together with various couples in the coming months and don't end up with one or more friendships good for a lifetime, try not to be discouraged. You'll have come away with experience in friendship building, and your life and faith will have touched other lives.

—Annette LaPlaca, *Today's Christian Woman*, November/December 1999

A: Friends count on each other, not just for fun and affirmation, but also for careful words of instruction and correction. Before addressing a difficult situation with a friend, though, check your motives. Honesty, especially when it comes to touchy subjects, must be accompanied by pure, loving motives. If your words aren't bathed in love, they'll hurt rather than heal.

Ask God to give you the right words and to take away any wrong motives. Then choose a time when you and your friend are alone and won't be interrupted. Begin by affirming your love and care for her. Then gently share your observation. Take care not to pass judgment or place blame. You might state your concern in "I" terms, such as: "I'm worried, Jill, that you've stopped taking your medicine. I think I see signs of your depression coming back."

Your friend's response to your words will tell you what to do next. If she becomes defensive, angry, or appears hurt, match your words to her response. If she's open, talk in greater depth about your concerns. However, if she clams up, back off. Give her a hug, tell her you're praying for her, and change the subject.

Topics that don't involve moral, health, or safety issues are best left alone. A friend who has gained ten pounds already knows it. She doesn't need you to point it out to her, regardless how helpful you think your words might be.

—Annette Smith, Today's Christian Woman, November/December 2002

Q: What do I say when a friend tells me she has had an abortion?

A: It's likely that someone you know has once had an abortion. She could be the woman who sits beside you at Bible study, your child's Sunday school teacher, or your best friend. So what do you do when a friend reveals this deep secret?

First, *accept and love her.* One of the best things you can do is to love your friend for who she is now and not reject her for what she did in her past. For women living with guilt and depression, speaking about the abortion can be the first step out of darkness into the light. But she'll talk only if she finds acceptance.

Second, *encourage her to get into a Christian support group for women who have had abortions.* There are many online resources, as well as post-abortive Bible studies, such as one titled "Forgiven and Set Free," by Linda Cochrane.

Third, listen *with your heart.* Don't try to fix your friend's problems or offer spiritual platitudes. Listen to her and walk with her through the recovery process. Yes, you'll hear pain, grief, and regret. But you don't have to be her counselor—just her confidante, encourager, and prayer partner.

—Gayle L. Gresham, *Today's Christian Woman*, January/February 2005

FRIENDS

Q: How should I respond to a friend who tells me she's gay?

A: God condemns homosexual behavior, not homosexual people. Because of His love for us, He prohibits behaviors He knows will harm us. We need to exemplify God's love for people. But how can you show God's love without approving of your friend's choice? It starts with considering your friend's needs before your own. What is she going through?

Instead of saying "How could you?" or "That's a sin," it's best to encourage your friend to talk. She may not have had a chance to process this with a believer. You might ask her, "How long have you been thinking about this?" "Have you told your family?" "How long do you think you've been a lesbian?" "What led you to think about homosexuality?" Listen carefully to the answers, exemplifying God's love.

Linda Schultz of Grace Unlimited says we don't have to compromise our belief in Scripture on the subject of homosexuality. Rather, we can simply agree to disagree. Schultz suggests saying, "One of us is wrong. So why not let the Holy Spirit be the one to let us know who is right?" Continue to pray for your friend, but don't tell her you're praying she won't be a lesbian. Say instead, "I'm praying God will show you what's best for your life."

—Marlo M. Schalesky, *Today's Christian Woman*, September/October 1999

Q: My friend is driving me crazy with her problems. What can I do?

A: High-maintenance friends pop up in everyone's life at one time or another. Whether it's her annoying habits or attitudes, a difficult husband, intolerable children, or overwhelming neediness, such friends can be trying. Here are solutions to pesky, high-maintenance friend problems:

• *The Frequent Phoner.* Set a time limit. When your friend calls, say, "I only have ten minutes to talk," then stick to that. Put on the oven timer. When it beeps, kindly let your friend know her time is up.

• *The Put-Down Complainer.* Listen for what's behind the complaint. Is it a lack of self-esteem that causes her to trash others? If so, you wouldn't be a genuine friend unless you gently pointed that out in an appropriate time and place.

• *The Problem Repeater.* If your friend's problems are continually the same, and she never does anything to change her situation, it may be time to say firmly, "It sounds as though you're struggling with the same issues. Have you considered professional counseling?" Help her find resources, then back off. If you don't, you only enable her to remain the victim.

• *The Uninvited Guest.* Don't always stop what you're doing when she lands at your doorstep. Say, "Hi! I'm in the middle of ironing. Want to grab a diet Coke and join me downstairs? We can talk while I work." By doing so, you're saying, "I want to be your friend, but I also need to get something done while you're here."

—Rhonda Rhea, *Today's Christian Woman*, March/April 2000

15

FRIENDS

Are You a High-Maintenance Friend?

1. You've just had another rough day at work and want to call your friend to vent but you remember she is having her in-laws over for dinner. You:
   - a. Call anyway. She'll understand.
   - b. Decide your friend has enough on her hands tonight. You'll touch base later.

2. Your friend has just discovered she's pregnant and shares her exciting news. You:
   - a. Scream in excitement and tell her you're taking her out to celebrate.
   - b. Say, "That's nice," then talk about when you first found out you were pregnant.

3. Your friend says something that rubs you the wrong way. You:
   - a. Refuse to talk to her for two weeks.
   - b. Swallow hard and take it, reasoning that she's your friend, and she'd never say something to intentionally hurt you.

4. You talk to your friend on the phone:
   - a. At least twice a day.
   - b. At least twice a week.

5. During a telephone conversation your friend says she needs to go. You:
   - a. Quickly wrap up and say good-bye.
   - b. Keep talking until she finally hangs up on you.

6. You promised to help your friend move. But then you're invited to a party. You:
   - a. Figure your friend will understand—and go to the party.
   - b. Remember how many times your friend has helped you, then help her move.

INSIGHT

7. Your friend doesn't connect with you as much as you'd like. You:
   a. Realize that as a mom of two kids she's probably overwhelmed and isn't connecting with anyone except Barney.
   b. Try to make her feel guilty by dropping little comments about how she's too busy to remember her friends.

8. You hate your job and keep complaining about it to your friend. She tries to cheer you up. You:
   a. Finally decide to do something about your situation.
   b. Do nothing, but keep complaining, figuring your friend will make you feel better.

9. You want to have lunch with your friend. She says she's busy but she'll check her schedule. You:
   a. Take that as a yes, then get mad when she can't make it.
   b. Tell her to give you a call when she has some free time.

10. Your friend tries to give you constructive feedback on a situation. You:
   a. Get upset, strongly defend yourself, and refuse to listen to her.
   b. Try to keep an open mind, realizing she might have a point.

FRIENDS

Scoring: 1. A=2, B=1; 2. A=1, B=2; 3. A=2, B=1; 4. A=2, B=1; 5. A=1, B=2; 6. A=2, B=1; 7. A=1, B=2; 8. A=1, B=2; 9. A=2, B=1; 10. A=2, B=1. Add up your score.

If you scored 10–12: You're a thoughtful friend. You take others' feelings into consideration and don't expect them to cater to your every need.

If you scored 13–16: Be careful not to expect too much from your friends. As Jesus said in Matthew 7:12: "Do to others what you would have them do to you." (NIV)

If you scored 17–20: Try putting more focus on the feelings of others. You'll find that people will be more willing to return the favor when they know you're interested in give-and-take.

—Leota Jeffrey, *Today's Christian Woman*, March/April 2000

Q: How do I handle feeling like I've lost something when one of my best friends gets married while I remain single?

A: First, realize that though your newly married friend still cares about you, you cannot be as high on her priority list anymore. Knowing this, you may be tempted to let the friendship go. This is a mistake. Even though your friend and her new husband will be making new friends with other couples and families, you can move ahead in your friendship with her under more flexible terms.

For instance, instead of enjoying frequent dinners together, do lunch together. Plan further ahead for big outings, such as a girls' weekend or a night on the town. E-mail may be a better way to stay in touch than long phone chats.

As you see your friend's life change, make changes in your own life. Do something you've always wanted to do, like taking a class or joining a new group. You may also benefit by moving closer to God. Sign up for e-mail devotionals and spend more time reading God's Word.

Your friend's new marriage can offer you glimpses of how she handles normal marriage issues. You get to see, hear, and learn what works and what doesn't work in a marriage. Hopefully, you can take that knowledge with you into your next relationship.

—Based on readers' responses, SinglesNewsletter@ChristianityToday.com, 2004

Q: How can I help my friend who is grieving?

A: It's difficult. You don't want to compound her pain by saying the wrong thing, yet you want to help lessen her suffering. So, recognizing that you can't fix the problem, you might try the following:

• *Be there.* A hug, a pat on the arm, or showing up at a memorial service is often as valued as anything else.

• *Listen.* Encourage your friend to talk about her loss. Pam Vredevelt, author of *Empty Arms*, says many women find it easier to suffer in silence after a miscarriage or stillbirth because others won't initiate discussions about their loss. So if your grieving friend says, "I don't know how I'm going to get out of bed tomorrow," ask her, "What's the scariest part of facing your day?" Then listen. Try responding in a way that allows your friend to express what she really feels.

• *Talk about the loved one.* Tell a grieving person how her loved one affected you, even if it was only minimally.

• *Share how you've reacted to loss.* Saying something such as "I remember when I felt as though I couldn't breathe, let alone eat," helps a friend know that others also feel that kind of pain. Be cautious, however, about saying "I understand how you feel"; some people might find this presumptuous. Every loss is different.

• *Follow through.* Grief doesn't end when a funeral is over. Send a card on the anniversary of someone's death or on what would have been a birthday or an anniversary. Don't worry about reminding your friend of the loss. The grief will always be there.

—Sheila Wray Gregoire, *Today's Christian Woman*, November/December 2000

10
Things to Do for a Grieving Friend

1. Pray for her—and tell her you're doing so.

2. Help her write thank-you cards.

3. Collect photos of the person who died and put them in an album.

4. Buy her a pretty journal.

5. Write out prayers for her and encourage others to do the same. Put these in a booklet and give it to her.

6. Give her money anonymously (funerals are expensive).

7. Pick up some basic groceries and deliver them to her.

8. Call her every week to check in.

9. Encourage her to go on walks or drives with you.

10. Keep inviting her to all the things you'd have invited her to before.

—Sheila Wray Gregoire, *Today's Christian Woman*, November/December 2000

Additional Resources

Books:

Born to Be Wild: Rediscover the Freedom of Fun,
Jill Baughan (New Hope, 2006)

Girlfriends' Getaway: A Complete Guide to the Weekend Adventure that Turns Friends into Sisters and Sisters into Friends, Elizabeth Butterfield and Kathleen Laing (Waterbrook, 2002)

Sisterchicks on the Loose,
Robin Jones Gunn (Multnomah, 2003)

The Daring Female's Guide to Ecstatic Living:
30 Dares for a More Gutsy and Fulfilling Life,
Natasha Kogan (Hyperion, 2006)

The Frazzled Female: Finding God's Peace in Your Daily Chaos,
Cindi Wood (B & H, 2006)

Chick Flicks: Dinner and a Movie—Friendship, Faith, and Fun
for Women's Groups (Group, 2006)

Websites:

www.todayschristianwoman.com
Great articles and resources for Christian women

www.christiananswers.net
Where you can go with your questions

www.shelovesgod.com
A Christian website for women to connect with other women

www.womenoffaith.com
Conferences and resources for women

Questions About

Health & Fitness

Q: Is stress ever a good thing? Sometimes I feel like I'm more productive when I'm juggling a variety of responsibilities.

A: Here are some tips on how to tap into the upside of stress in your life:

1. *Hire a "stress manager."* Ask a trusted friend to hold you accountable for maintaining a healthy balance in your life. Share your goals and calendar with her. Then determine checkpoints—weekly or monthly meetings when she can see how you're maintaining your schedule. Give her permission to nudge you back on track if necessary.

2. *Adjust your attitude.* Often the way we size up a demanding situation determines whether the stress we experience serves as our ally or our enemy. "Assume a positive viewpoint," suggests Dennis E. Hensley, author of *Positive Workaholism.* "Rather than saying 'No one will hire me for this job because I'm too old,' a senior applicant can adjust her attitude and say, 'I have more experience than anyone else interviewing for this job.'"

3. *Ignite the spark.* World-class athletes clamp headsets over their ears as they wait their turn to compete. Whether they're listening to a favorite motivational speaker or a tape of inspirational music isn't important. What matters is that they've identified their personal strategy for pumping them-selves up and getting their butterflies to fly in formation.

4. *Give yourself time.* One key to harnessing positive stress is allowing time to prepare for demanding situations and time to rejuvenate between them. As you study the month ahead, try to equalize your obligations.

5. *Exercise.* Exercise rids us of tension and refreshes us. What kind of exercise is best? The country's leading fitness activity is also its simplest: walking.

—Holly G. Miller, *Today's Christian Woman,* July/August 1998

Tips for Getting Fit

Here are five things you can do daily to improve your well-being.

1. *Avoid falling for fitness-revolution hype.* Between unrealistic body types, skimpy clothing, and all the machines purporting to keep you fit, there are many reasons to feel discouraged. Observe fitness industry images with detachment; remind yourself the best reason to exercise is to stay healthy, and you have everything you need to be physically active.

2. *Keep track of your efforts.* Record your activity so you can fine-tune your approach to exercise by discovering what works for you.

3. *Make deals with yourself.* When you don't have the desire to tackle a twenty-minute walk, give yourself permission to do five minutes to let yourself off the hook. Usually a five-minute walk will turn into a twenty-minute one. Getting started is the most important step toward physical activity as a way of life.

4. *Find a fitness professional.* It's possible to hire a qualified trainer without breaking the bank. Most can design a safe and effective exercise program for you, work with you for a few sessions, then follow up when needed. Try to find a fitness professional with certification from ACSM (the American College of Sports Medicine), NASM (the National Academy of Sports Medicine), ACE (American Council on Exercise), or another nationally recognized fitness trainer organization.

5. *Make exercise enjoyable.* Choose an activity you look forward to doing; otherwise, it won't become a consistent part of your life.

—Ruth McGinnis, *Today's Christian Woman*, September/October 2002

INSIGHT

Q: I take antidepressants for depression and anxiety. However, many of my Christian friends suggest I'm just popping pills to solve my problems. Why do believers make people feel guilty for taking medication for depression?

A: Such reactions often are based on ignorance or misunderstanding. Many people don't understand what clinical depression is or how utterly debilitating it can be. They mistakenly think it's a case of the blues, and that if you just prayed more and pushed yourself more, you'd be fine.

People who don't understand what depression is seem to assume that medication to treat something with an emotional component is wrong, except when a clear organic cause is discovered. But the mind-body connection is so complex that such black-and-white thinking leads to gross oversimplification.

When biological signs accompany the psychological aspects of depression, research has shown the most effective treatment is a combination of psychological and medical attention. God graciously has enabled people to discover medications that alleviate much human suffering, depression included.

At the same time, it's important to note that taking medication alone usually isn't effective. Other actions can aid in recovery. Just as someone with arthritis takes medication and follows an exercise regimen, someone who is depressed may not only require medication but also a Christian counselor to help her work through thoughts and feelings that feed the depression.

—Diane Mandt Langberg, *Today's Christian Woman*, September/October 2004.

Q: I'm 27, married, and the mom of four. When I was a teen, I battled bulimia and anorexia. Although I feel God cured me of my eating disorders, now that I'm trying to lose the weight I gained after four pregnancies, I'm concerned I may relapse. Is this common?

A: It is. After all, you're probably tempted to find a shortcut to a pre-pregnancy body after having four babies in short succession. It's also possible that with four young ones to care for, your life feels a little out of control. Attempting to control your weight may be one way you relieve your anxiety about that.

I encourage you to think about what function an eating disorder serves for you. Understanding its purpose will help you battle it more effectively. For example, when you were a teen, the odds are high that your eating disorder had more to do with some other issue than simply your body weight. I suspect whatever that was has cropped up again and needs your attention.

Since you don't want to model eating-disorder behaviors for your watching children, keep yourself from getting locked into this destructive pattern again. If the struggle intensifies or you begin to fall back into old habits, seek help in the ways that benefited you before—counseling or a support group.

—Diane Mandt Langberg, *Today's Christian Woman*, September/October 2004

Q: I have read a lot about Attention Deficit Hyperactivity Disorder (ADHD/ADD) for kids, but I'm starting to wonder if I might suffer from this too. No matter how hard I try, my life is always spinning out of control. I'm constantly late to appointments, and I forget important commitments. On top of it all, I feel depressed and unable to muster the energy to keep all these plates spinning. Could I have ADHD?

A: You very well might have this disorder. For years, society thought only children suffered from Attention Deficit Hyperactivity Disorder (ADHD/ADD), which affects about 20 million Americans. However, studies now show that about two to three percent of adults are likely to suffer with ADHD's effects—and up to fifty percent of those adults are women.

The majority of these women have ADD—Attention Deficit Disorder without the hyperactivity—and are often misdiagnosed as depressed, since depression is one of its symptoms. Many sufferers don't think they have ADD because they believe high levels of stress and disorganization are the norm in our fast-paced culture. But those who have ADD suffer from constant, severe stress and disorganization, as you've described. I have this problem. Some people have found relief through medications such as Ritalin. But this hasn't been an option for me because I've been either pregnant or breastfeeding for the last ten years. I've learned, though, there are physiological factors I can control. Out of necessity, I've developed coping strategies.

First, I've started taking better care of myself. On days when my brain is feeling foggy, I ask myself three basic questions: Have I eaten right? Did I get enough sleep? Do I need to exercise? Certainly good nutrition, adequate sleep, and physical activity are essential for everyone, but they can make a noticeable difference in a person with ADD.

I also begin my devotional time with a few pages of journal writing and prayer. During this time, God often reveals strategies to help manage my day. While organization and time-management are difficult for people with ADD, what I lack in internal structure, I make up for with external helpers. Every day I make a list of the essentials I must accomplish. Sometimes following the list is the only way I keep from wandering aimlessly around.

Besides my list, I use a daily planner and carry it wherever I go. I often jot my responsibilities into time slots in my planner, then set an alarm to remind me to change activities. I've also found it helps to set my watch and car clock ahead ten minutes to trick myself into arriving places on time.

Although the term *Attention Deficit Disorder* sometimes makes me squirm, I've decided that having ADD need not be a liability in my life. Rather, my creativity and periods of intense attentiveness have allowed me to do things I might not have done otherwise, such as professional storytelling. With structure and God's grace, I'm making peace with ADD.

—Katherine G. Bond, *Today's Christian Woman*, November/December 2000

ADD/ADHD Checklist

Do you have ADHD or ADD? Ask yourself if any of the following are true of you:

- You have trouble sustaining attention.
- You make careless mistakes and don't pay attention to detail.
- You tune out during conversations, lectures, sermons.
- You have difficulty keeping track of schedules.
- You constantly are losing things, such as your purse, papers, keys.
- You can't remain still; you're physically restless, fidgety.
- You have trouble completing projects and jump from one activity to another.
- You were told by parents and teachers you should have tried harder in school.
- You are frequently forgetful.
- You are frequently rushing, overcommitted, or late.
- You make impulsive decisions or purchases.
- You frequently blurt something out before you think.
- You feel overwhelmed and disorganized in your daily life.
- You are easily distracted from the task you are doing.
- You go off on tangents in conversations.
- You tend to interrupt.
- You have trouble balancing your checkbook or doing paperwork.

Having difficulty with one or two of these things doesn't mean you
have ADHD. However, if you responded "yes" to several,
you may want to seek help from a qualified health professional.

—Ginger McFarland, *Today's Christian Woman*, November/December 2000

Get Help with an ADD Coach

ADD coaching is a one-on-one, non-therapeutic intervention for managing ADD symptoms. Like a personal trainer, the ADD coach is equal parts listener, cheerleader, teacher, and standards-keeper. First, a coach helps a client identify goals and values. Then she develops individualized systems for organizing, following through on tasks, or managing time. Unlike most consultants, an ADD coach provides high levels of emotional support and accountability through frequent, ongoing contact.

For example, if you or your spouse needs a system for paying bills, a coach might suggest the use of a calendar with pockets. Bills and time-sensitive items can be tucked in an appropriate date to keep them from being lost or overlooked. In addition, your coach might encourage you or your family member to deal with any correspondence at the same time every day.

Coaches work over the phone, by fax or online service, at the workplace or in the home, depending on your needs or preferences. Some clients prefer short, daily phone appointments, while others gain more from longer, less frequent contact or in-person sessions.

Coaching can be an excellent complement to medication and counseling in an overall ADD/ADHD treatment program. To learn more about ADHD and ADD coaching, check your local library, ask your healthcare provider, or visit www.add.org.

—Amy Chapin, *Today's Christian Woman*, November/December 2000

INSIGHT

Q: I am extremely overweight. For years I've been considering undergoing bariatric (gastric bypass) surgery to take off the excess pounds. As a Christian, am I wrong for considering this extreme measure to improve my body?

A: Surgery for weight loss is extreme, but it's the most effective tool we have right now. As Christians, we have a responsibility to ourselves and to our children to be good stewards of our minds, spirits, and bodies. Surgery can be an act of good stewardship of the body for believers who are morbidly obese.

Before I'll agree to perform bariatric surgery, our patients are required to attend an orientation session where they learn about different types of weight-loss surgery and the advantages and disadvantages of each. They are also expected to attend a support-group meeting so they can meet other patients who have had weight-loss surgery. In addition to consultation with the surgeon, they have a comprehensive physical exam by the primary-care physician, consultation with a psychologist, and consultation with a nutritionist.

Certain medical problems prohibit a patient from having surgery, such as severe heart or pulmonary (lung) disease that isn't expected to improve with weight loss, metastatic cancer (cancer that already has spread to other parts of the body), and mental or emotional problems that wouldn't allow a patient to handle the stress and lifestyle changes following surgery.

There are a variety of emotional problems as well. Some people have a difficult time dealing with the lifestyle changes after surgery. Dietary change is especially difficult for emotional eaters. Some people have relationship problems, especially after they lose the weight. Many of these problems are present before the surgery but become exaggerated with the stress and with the changes that take place after surgery. That's why it's so important to talk with a psychologist before surgery—to minimize or eliminate these problems.

It's important for patients to have close follow-up with their surgeon, so the doctor can monitor their progress with weight loss and improvement of health conditions. All patients should expect to be on vitamin supplements for life, because after the surgery, no matter how well they eat, their body doesn't absorb certain vitamins and minerals the same.

Even though surgery is a lot to go through and can have significant complications, it makes such a dramatic improvement in the quality of life for morbidly obese people that, in the end, most are very happy with the decision they've made.

—Dr. Lana G. Nelson, *Today's Christian Woman*. May/June 2005

Q: I hear so much about bone density loss. I'm only in my thirties. Do I need to be concerned about this problem?

A: Building strong bones early in life and continuing healthy habits will keep your frame strong. Here's how to start:

• *Indulge in calcium-rich foods.* Calcium is readily available in: skim milk (8 ounces = 300 mg); low-fat yogurt (8 ounces = 400–450 mg); cheese (1 ounce = 150–250 mg); broccoli or other dark green leafy vegetables such as kale, bok choy, and collard or turnip greens (1 cup = 100–190 mg); tofu processed with calcium-sulfate (1/2 cup = 250 mg); salmon (2 ounces canned = 125 mg); almonds (1 ounce = 80 mg).

• *Take your vitamins.* Healthy bones also need a consistent supply of nutrients such as magnesium, potassium, vitamins B-6, B-12, folic acid, and vitamins K and D.

• *Avoid calcium drainers.* Excessive caffeine, salt, and animal protein markedly increase calcium loss. Colas (regular or diet) and processed foods that contain high levels of phosphorus, sugar, and the artificial sweetener Aspartame also block the body's ability to absorb calcium. Chlorinated, fluoridated tap water is a reducer of bone mass, so bone up on bottled water when you can. Finally, limit your use of antacids. Calcium is absorbed through the hydrochloric acid found in your stomach. Antacids reduce that acid, so the calcium you may take with it has a more difficult time reaching your bones.

• *Exercise regularly.* Bones are strengthened by having muscles pull on them. Weight-bearing exercises such as brisk walking or jogging, in-line skating, tennis, or low-impact and step aerobics are best.

—Cheri Fuller, *Today's Christian Woman*, January/February 2000

Are You at Risk for Osteoporosis?

You may be a candidate for bone loss if:

- You're thin or small-boned
- Have a family history of osteoporosis
- Are postmenopausal
- Use steroid medications such as Prednisone
- Don't exercise or lift weights
- Strenuously exercise to the point of stopping menstruation
- Are either Caucasian or Asian
- Have a low-calcium/vitamin D diet
- Smoke

Whether or not you're at risk for osteoporosis, most women after age 35 need calcium supplements because it's hard to get enough calcium by diet alone. Be aware of the needs of different ages. Young women ages 13 to 19 need 1,200 to 1,500 mg of calcium, and women ages 20 to 45 need at least 1,000 mg daily. Pregnant moms need 1,500 mg; nursing moms need 2,000 mg; and women over 45, need 1,500 mg.

Just taking a calcium supplement won't prevent you from losing bone. The calcium must be absorbed. But calcium supplements exist in different combinations with different concentrations and absorption capabilities. How do you know which one to choose? One simple method for testing a particular brand of calcium supplement is to place it in a glass of white vinegar at full strength and make sure it breaks up within thirty minutes.

—Ginger McFarland, *Today's Christian Woman*, January/February 2000

INSIGHT

Q: Recently, I saw my doctor after experiencing severe abdominal pain. He said I might have endometriosis. What is this, and should I be worried?

A: If you have endometriosis, you're not alone. More than 5 million women and girls of all ages in North America have been diagnosed with endometriosis.

Endometriosis derives its name from the endometrial tissue that lines the uterus. This tissue normally builds up each month then sheds during a woman's menstrual cycle. In women who have endometriosis, endometrial tissue (or tissue like it) grows outside the uterus in the form of lesions, implants, nodules, and cysts. These become inflamed and painful because this misplaced tissue has no way of leaving the body.

Most often endometrial tissue grows on the ovaries, fallopian tubes, and in the lining of the pelvic cavity, but can also spread to the bladder and intestines, and occasionally in areas outside the abdomen. Endometriosis can cause scar tissue, adhesions, and intestinal obstructions as it grows and spreads, compressing and sometimes even invading surrounding organs.

Since the symptoms of endometriosis can mimic other diseases such as appendicitis, ovarian cysts, and bowel and colon diseases, it's best not to assume one has endometriosis until a definitive diagnosis has been made. This can only be done through laparoscopy, a procedure that's usually done as outpatient surgery with a general anesthetic.

While endometriosis will probably not be life threatening, it can lead to other health complications. So be sure to see a gynecologist who can test further to see if you have endometriosis and can determine how best to treat it.

—Joanna Bloss, *Today's Christian Woman*, March/April 2004

Q: Last year I underwent a painful divorce. My kids got into all kinds of trouble at school. My company moved its location, so now I have to drive an hour each way for work. I feel like my life is in shambles. It's like I'm struggling to put one foot in front of the other. Why can't I snap out of this funk?

A: Sounds like you might be suffering from depression. This isn't surprising, given the challenges you've been facing. Depression can be brought on by genetic factors or external triggers, like divorce, job changes, major loss or disappointment, prolonged chronic illness, and certain prescription medications.

I used to have the misconception that depression could be cured solely with perseverance, optimism, and prayer. But recent medical research reveals there are real, measurable reasons why people become depressed. Researchers have learned that when there's an insufficient level of the neurotransmitter serotonin in the frontal lobes of the brain, depressive symptoms appear (neuro-transmitters are chemicals that allow cells to communicate with each other in the brain). A chemically based depression can last for months, years, or—without treatment—a lifetime. Several studies also have shown a family depression connection.

Not everyone experiences the same symptoms you've described. Some people may have trouble keeping themselves presentable, cry uncontrollably, exhibit extreme anxiety, fear, or worry. Often clinical depression is masked by other behaviors such as alcoholism or drug use.

The key to overcoming depression is finding the right counselors to help you determine the best way out of the pit. Treatment options can differ from one person to the next, but hope and healing are possible.

—Cheryl K. Ewings, *Today's Christian Woman*, November/December 1999

Depressed—or Just Blue?

Symptoms of Depression:

- Sleeping all the time or not at all

- Drastic increase or decrease in appetite

- Crying frequently for no apparent reason

- Loss of interest in things that formerly interested you

  - Symptoms lasting more than a couple weeks

    Other possible conditions to rule out:

    - Premenstrual Syndrome

    - Thyroid imbalance

    - Low blood sugar

  - Anemia

- Seasonal Affective Disorder (depression triggered by lack of sunlight)

Look for a qualified professional to help you identify whether you have depression, then find ways to treat it. To find the right person for you, first, ask for a personal referral. Ideally, try to get a recommendation from a therapist's client. If you can't find that, ask your doctor or pastor for a few names. Look for a licensed psychologist, social worker, or family therapist who shares your values and faith (psychiatrists typically don't do much counseling).

Next, visit a therapist or two. After your first visit, ask yourself: Did I feel heard? Did I feel valued? Did I feel comfortable with this therapist? If you answer no to any of these, keep searching for the right fit.

Then check out the cost. Is this counselor covered by your insurance policy? Is the cost doable? Typically, psychologists are most expensive, followed by social workers and family therapists. Is the office location convenient for you?

Along with the therapy, do what you can to get back into good health patterns:

- Exercise

- Improve your nutrition

- Take multiple vitamins with iron

- Get involved with a support group in the church or community

- Take herbal supplements such as St. John's Wort

- If your doctor suggests it, take an antidepressant

—Linda Eiserloh, *Today's Christian Woman*, November/December 1999

Q: I always seem to be tired. How can I go from feeling sluggish to being more energized each day?

A: Sleep is essential for rebuilding your body. Ideally, you should be able to wake up without an alarm clock. If you're constantly jerked out of a deep sleep by the alarm or if you usually feel drowsy during the day, you need more sleep. Try these sleep-friendly habits.

• Establish a firm bedtime. Since my alarm goes off at 5:45 a.m., I try to start my bedtime preparations at 9:30 p.m., and settle into bed by 10:00 p.m. A set bedtime makes it easier to turn off the TV, another prime sleep-snatcher.

• Allow time to wind down. Sipping a cup of herbal tea or warm milk before bed can soothe frazzled nerves or an over-wired body. Others find a warm soak in the tub for ten or fifteen minutes an hour before bedtime works wonders.

• Even our best efforts to catch some sleep can be for naught if we eat or drink the wrong thing too close to bedtime. Coffee is a known sleep-killer; so are hot chocolate and regular tea.

Other simple diet tips help ward off tiredness. Loading ourselves up on chips, sweets, and other non-nutritive foods will do nothing for our energy, not to mention our waistlines. And we should get plenty of water. Mild dehydration can cause fatigue. I notice a real difference in the way I feel depending on whether or not I'm getting the recommended six to eight glasses (that's eight-ounce glasses—roughly a half gallon). So give these ideas a try. They may provide the energy boost you need.

—Deborah R. Simon, *Today's Christian Woman*, November/December 1998

Q: I have been trying to lose ten pounds. I walk nearly every day and watch every morsel of food I eat. Still, the scale never seems to budge. Am I destined to remain overweight?

A: Like you, I walked regularly and dieted faithfully, but I got discouraged that I wasn't losing more weight. Then I discovered weight lifting. After just a few weeks of incorporating this into my fitness regimen, I started seeing results. Here are some reasons why strength training's worth the effort:

1. *It maximizes calorie burn.* As you build muscle and lose fat, your body burns calories more efficiently.

2. *It makes you look thinner.* Increased muscle and decreased fat mean that even if your scale doesn't change, your shape does.

3. *It strengthens your bones.* You can fight osteoporosis. One of your primary weapons is strength training, along with a diet rich in calcium and vitamin D.

4. *It helps prevent disease.* Studies show strength training helps lower blood pressure and bad cholesterol levels, as well as minimizes some risks associated with Type 2 diabetes. It also may help prevent certain types of cancer.

5. *It reduces back pain and gives you better posture.* Weight training strengthens and tones abdominal and back muscles, making them strong and flexible.

6. *It improves sleep and gives you more energy.* People who exercise fall asleep more quickly, sleep more deeply, awaken less often, and sleep longer than those who don't.

—Joanna Bloss, *Today's Christian Woman*, September/October 2005

Q: I used to think that women were more likely to die of breast cancer than anything else. But recently, I heard that women are much more likely to die of heart disease than breast cancer. Is this true? What should I know about heart disease?

A: Women are ten times more likely to die of cardiovascular disease than breast cancer. Cardiovascular disease is the number-one killer among women.

As a medical student I was taught the classic symptoms of a heart attack are crushing chest pain associated with shortness of breath, sweating, and a feeling of impending doom. Those are the classic symptoms for men. But recent research shows that the most common symptom women experience isn't chest pain but shortness of breath. So if you routinely climb two flights of stairs at work with no problem, and you start noticing that halfway up those stairs you have to stop and rest because you're short of breath, that may be a symptom of heart disease.

Sleep disturbances are very common in the weeks leading up to a heart attack. Many women also complain of unusual fatigue.

Your risks for a heart attack increase as you age, and if you have a history of heart disease in your family. Other controllable factors include smoking, high blood pressure, abnormal levels of blood cholesterol, a sedentary lifestyle, and obesity.

Aside from not smoking and staying away from secondhand smoke, the key is a heart-healthy diet and regular exercise. Eat colorful fruits, vegetables, and whole grains. Meat, including poultry, should be used as a condiment, not as a main entrée. Use olive oil as the main source of your fat calories.

—Corrie Cutrer, *Today's Christian Woman*, March/April 2007

Check-Up Times

	If you're 20 to 39	40 to 49	50 and older
Pelvic exam	annually	annually	annually
Pap test	annually until you've had 3 satisfactory tests, then at your doctor's discretion	annually until you've had 3 satisfactory tests, then at your doctor's discretion	annually until you've had 3 satisfactory tests, then at your doctor's discretion
Clinical breast exam	3 years	annually	annually
Breast self-exam	monthly	monthly	monthly
Mammogram	doctor's recommendation only	1-2 years	annually
Skin exam	3 years	annually	annually
Skin self-exam	monthly	monthly	monthly
Blood pressure	2 years	2 years	2 years
Cholesterol *(total and HDL)*	5 years	5 years	5 years; 3-5 years if 65 and older
Eye exam	at least 1 between puberty and age 40	2–4 years	2–4 years; 1–2 years if 65 or older
Tetanus booster	10 years	10 years	10 years
Fasting plasma glucose *(diabetes) test*	doctor's recommendation only	3 years after age 45	3 years

—*Today's Christian Woman*, September/October 1999

Q: My teen complains about her health a lot. It seems like she's always sick with something. How do I know if she's just faking or if there's a real issue that needs attention?

A: While it may seem like your teen is becoming a hypochondriac, consider the following:

1. *Your adolescent's body is maturing and developing.* Increased body awareness can cause various aches and pains similar to the symptoms of a cold and the flu.

2. *Teens still lack the insight to understand fully what's going on inside them.* Ask your teen what she is feeling, both physically and emotionally. What's going on at school or with friends? Reassure her that her symptoms are perfectly normal, and explain that emotional stresses often work their way out physically.

3. *Sometimes the pain is a cry for attention.* According to Allen McKinnon, a pediatrician and family counselor in Wisconsin, teens on the brink of independence are sometimes fearful, and feeling sick is a safe way to ask for extra attention from Mom or Dad. Plan some one-on-one time with your teen when she's not sick.

4. *Don't forget the power of prayer.* Tell your teen that prayer helps in times of stress and physical pain. Ask God to intervene and heal, acknowledging that we need His help to get better. Pray Philippians 4:6–7 with her: "Do not be anxious about anything, but in everything, by prayer and petition, with thanksgiving, present your requests to God. And the peace of God, which transcends all understanding, will guard your hearts and your minds in Christ Jesus" (NIV).

—Lisa Jackson, *Christian Parenting Today*, March/April 2002

Additional Resources

Books:

The Anxiety Cure: A Proven Method for Dealing with Worry, Stress, and Panic Attacks,
Dr. Archibald D. Hart (Thomas Nelson, 2001)

Empowering Your Health,
Dr. Asa Andrew (Thomas Nelson, 2007)

100 Days of Weight Loss: the Secret to Being Successful on Any Diet Plan,
Linda Spangle (Thomas Nelson, 2007)

Total Heart Health for Women: A Life-Enriching Plan for Physical and Spiritual Well Being,
Dr. Ed. B. Young (Thomas Nelson, 2007)

Thrilled to Death: How the Endless Pursuit of Pleasure Is Leaving us Numb,
Dr. Archibald D. Hart (Thomas Nelson, 2007)

What Have You Got to Lose? Experience a Richer Life by Letting Go of the Things that Confuse, Clutter, and Contaminate, Stephen Arterburn (Thomas Nelson, 2007)

Living Well with Endometriosis: What Your Doctor Doesn't Tell You that You Need to Know,
Kerry-Ann Morris (Collins, 2006)

Websites:

www.add.org Attention Deficit Disorder

www.adaa.org Anxiety Disorders Association of America (ADAA)

www.nimh.nih.gov National Institute of Mental Health (NIMH)

www.ivillage.com iVillage health channel

www.acefitness.org American Council on Exercise

www.ruthmcginnis.com Wellness information from Ruth McGinnis

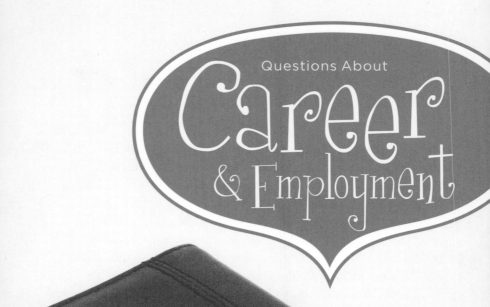

Questions About

Career
& Employment

Q: I believe that God has a particular work in mind for each person, but how do I know if a certain job is my calling? And how can I find meaning and purpose in my job when I am just working to pay the bills?

A: Christians in the workplace often wonder if what they do has eternal value or significance. We take heart that in Christ all work is redeemed and transformed. Virtually every job or profession is a good and noble calling from God and can reflect a divine purpose or intent for the world. Healthcare professionals, for example, reflect God as Healer and Great Physician. Teachers and educators convey God's wisdom and learning. Farmers, grocery store clerks, restaurateurs, cooks, and waiters participate in God's good work to feed the hungry. Architects, builders, contractors, and real estate agents help people gain needed shelter. Consider your own job and line of work. How might your work reflect some aspect of God's character?

Some people may be called to be accountants or policy analysts; others may be called to operate a forklift or manage a mutual fund. Two people in the same job may have entirely different understandings of why God has called them to that role. But all of us can nevertheless be called.

How do we know if we're called? While no pat answers exist, we can discern a sense of calling through the affirmation of trusted counsel and friends as well as our own experience of our work. We are most likely to sense God's call and feel His pleasure when we are using our gifts and abilities in areas that line up with who God created us to be.

Ultimately, seeing one's work as a calling depends on discerning the voice of the One who calls—and that is a matter of knowing God and learning to recognize His voice. We can be called to be a cook or a forest ranger or a policy analyst or hospice nurse or take a role in virtually any other field if we do it as a reflection of God's good work in the world and experience it as a satisfying expression of who He created us to be. The more we understand how God created us and how He thinks and loves, the more we will sense that we are doing what He has called us to do.

Q: My job puts me under such stress. Is there some way to reduce the tension and make the most of my job situation?

A: With the hindsight of thirty-five years in the marketplace, I've learned no one has a perfect job. But I've also discovered that there are alternate ways to handle the inevitable workplace conflicts or stresses that we encounter. And the only person whose cooperation these strategies require is your own. So try the following.

1. Identify the real problem: Is it you? Some job stress is self-inflicted. When you clarify exactly what the issue is behind your workplace stress, it can lessen your sense of victimization, even if the revelation isn't particularly welcome.

Self-check: What is the main source of my work-related stress? How am I contributing to the problem?

2. Take charge of your attitude. How many times have you sat in the employee lunchroom with coworkers when a person starts to complain about a change in the office hours, the vacation schedule, or the telephone rotation? Complaining, or venting, gives the appearance of relief. But rehashing a stressful situation in a setting that offers no opportunity for correcting the problem takes emotional energy and doesn't change the problem. It can also make a problem seem worse than it is.

Self-check: Who is the appropriate person with whom to discuss this problem? Is there another way I can look at this situation? What can I do to help eliminate this stress rather than rehash it?

3. Sort out what can and can't change. If you love clear instructions and an even flow of work, then working in an advertising agency or a sales office full of hard-charging free spirits is migraine material. Since it's doubtful that your environment is going to change, any change must take place in you.

Self-check: What's within my power to change about my situation? If nothing changes, can I stay and still be true to myself as God created me? If I should leave, what needs to happen for me to be prepared?

4. Live in the present. Stress is more manageable if it doesn't also carry the weight of any past and future problems that bear any resemblance to it. For example, if you find yourself saying: "My boss always waits until the last minute to do these mailings" or "My team leader never asks my opinion," realize that piling everything but the kitchen sink onto your problem sabotages solutions by sheer pound weight.

Self-check: Has piling up problems ever solved anything? Whom can I ask to hold me accountable for changing this behavior pattern? Am I willing to deal with my present situation without attaching baggage to it?

—Verla Gillmor, *Today's Christian Woman*, November/December 1999

Q: Every day when my husband and I get home from work, we seem to end up in one-upmanship over whose day was harder. Why can't I tell my husband about my day without it turning into a competition?

A: Of all the people in our lives, the spouse is the one whose appreciation we most need. If we don't receive the recognition we need and want, we start devising strategies to get it. Unfortunately, those attempts often come across as trying to make ourselves appear harder working or more put-upon than our spouse. A couple of guidelines may help curb your competition:

1. *Be alert and responsive to pleas for encouragement.* If your spouse expresses frustration with preparing the month-end reports or enduring a coworker's inefficiency, try not to counter with something like, "Well, at my job . . ." What your spouse may need most is assurance that he can handle the challenge.

2. *Express appreciation.* Remember to praise your spouse, whether at home or at the office. "You finished the month-end reports—let's celebrate!" Assigning certain roles to each gender doesn't give us permission to take each other for granted. For a wife who comes home from her day job and immediately starts taking charge of the household, a word of acknowledgment and recognition from her husband will mean a great deal, even if she believes that domestic responsibilities are rightly hers. Similarly, a husband who takes seriously his role as breadwinner and works hard to succeed likes to know that his spouse values his efforts.

—Alicia Howe, *Marriage Partnership*, Winter 1998

Q: My coworker just got the promotion I was in line to receive. I should be happy for her, but instead I feel jealous. I'm ashamed to admit that career envy is eating me alive. How do I get this green-eyed monster to go away?

A: Rather than feeling ashamed that envy is alive in you, be grateful you are recognizing it as the sin it is. Women who have experienced the same battle with professional jealousy say that the first step to overcoming it is confessing it as sin and praying about it. The freedom and release of prayerful confession sets you free to move to the next step.

Next, rejoice. The surest solution for feeling down is looking up. When a colleague succeeds, celebrate with her. I keep a stack of postcards ready to send out when I hear about someone's success. The postage stamps are already on them so I can't change my mind after I've written, "Way to go, my friend!"

If you're not in the spotlight, count your blessings, including the freedom to not have all the answers. Many a career or ministry has collapsed under too much, too soon. Try to relax with the tasks you've been given rather than longing for something bigger, better, or faster.

Sometimes when you're worn out, negative emotions such as envy can take a foothold. Taking good care of yourself is good insurance against a roving green eye.

Comparisons are never productive unless Christ is the mirror. He is the one who is jealous for us, desiring that our whole heart, mind, body, and soul be focused on Him.

—Liz Curtis Higgs, *Today's Christian Woman*, October 1997

Q: Gossip is a prevalent problem among my coworkers. What can I do to avoid the office rumor mill?

A: Human resources specialist Cassie Dibiase, owner of Resources and Results Consulting in Houston, Texas, says gossip is probably the single, most destructive behavior in the workplace. Consider these key points:

• Workplace gossips are viewed as untrustworthy and are less likely to receive promotions or key assignments.

• Important lines of communication between employees and supervisors often are disrupted because of the lack of trust created by gossip.

• What might appear to be simple gossip often can result in a full-blown investigation, causing irreparable damage to an individual's reputation and to the gossiper's reputation.

• A good rule of thumb to help you determine whether you're gossiping: Ask yourself how you'd feel if the person you're discussing suddenly entered your conversation. Would you be embarrassed? Chances are, you know when you're gossiping. You get that unsettled feeling from the Holy Spirit that says what you're discussing isn't appropriate.

• Changing the subject is a great way to cut gossip before it goes any further. Better still, turn to your gossiping coworker and ask what's happening in her life. Getting her to talk about herself is almost guaranteed to change the conversation.

—Rhonda Wilson, *Today's Christian Woman*, November/December 2005

Q: My job occasionally requires that I travel out of town with a male coworker. My husband is uncomfortable with the situation; he finds it difficult to believe men and women can be just friends. I love my husband and would never think of straying—but I also have a job to do. What do you feel is appropriate for this type of situation?

A: Your husband's concerns aren't without basis. While some men and women can remain "just friends," many others have shipwrecked their marriages on those words. It's easy for a friendship or business relationship to change in a split second by the touch of a hand.

You need to talk this issue over with your husband. If you were to stay in this job, what actions would help him feel you're safeguarding your marriage? Are there specific things he finds threatening, such as your having dinners with this man? Are you in touch with your husband while you're gone? Does he know your coworker and interact with him? Lay down some guidelines together, then be sure you honor them.

It's possible that no amount of discussion will allay your husband's fears. If that's the case, you'll be faced with a tough decision. If you love your work, you'll find it hard to let go—and the temptation to choose work will be as strong as the temptation to release it and be bitter or angry with your husband. But remember that your marriage is based on a vow before God, and your job is not. This isn't about job versus marriage; it's about your marriage.

—Diane Mandt, *Today's Christian Woman*, July/August 1998

Q: How do I know if a coworker's actions are considered sexual harassment, and what can I do if they are?

A: Title VII of the Civil Rights Act of 1964 identifies sexual harassment as unwanted, repeated sexual attention at work. It is illegal. A partial list of actions that may constitute sexual harassment includes inappropriate gifts, unwelcome hugging or touching, sharing intimate details of one's sexual life, sexual anecdotes, sexual innuendos, excessive personal compliments (especially about appearance), and overt behavior such as stalking. If you think you're being sexually harassed:

1. *Ask questions.* To learn about the law in your state, call the U.S. Equal Employment Opportunities Commission (800-669-4000) and ask for the office nearest you. Also obtain counseling, information, and even free legal advice through 9 to 5, a nonprofit organization that helps working women with problems on the job (800-522-0925).

2. *Say no.* Clearly communicate your disapproval. Don't smile or apologize; that sends a confusing signal.

3. *Name the behavior.* Whatever your coworker does that's inappropriate, say the specific words for it out loud. That often stops the behavior immediately.

4. *Put it in writing.* If speaking to the person is too uncomfortable, write a letter identifying the objectionable behavior. State your feelings about it and make it clear that you expect it to stop. Keep a dated copy of your letter.

5. *Enlist others.* If previous attempts to deal directly with your harasser fail, get others involved. Most companies have a policy for dealing with sexual harassment.

6. *Keep records.* Matthew 18:17 offers a final guideline: Consider going public. To prepare for this, log all incidents involving your harasser. Be specific about words and actions used; the date, time, and place; and those who may have witnessed the incident. Photocopy any offensive materials such as cartoons or memos. Evidence is important if you decide to file a complaint. Obtain copies of your work records, and keep them at home. Whenever you have a performance review, be sure to get a copy of it to add to your home file.

7. *Consider legal options.* File a formal complaint with the Fair Employment Practice Agency or the Equal Employment Opportunity Commission. File within 180 days after the incident. Experts recommend retaining an attorney when you first decide to make your complaint. Even if you haven't confronted your harasser, you may be eligible for compensation for lost wages and benefits, attorney fees, injunctive relief (changes in workplace policy), or punitive damages.

—Ginger Kolbaba, *Today's Christian Woman,* November/December 2001

Q: I had an office romance with a coworker, and it didn't pan out. Unfortunately, our jobs dictate that we still have to interact with each other. I'm uncomfortable because I wasn't the one who ended the relationship. How can I remain professional while working with this guy?

A: It's not easy to work with someone when you're struggling with a wounded heart. But while you're on the mend, separate the professional from the emotional components as clearly as you can. Do you need to talk about the relationship? Of course! Doing so helps you heal. But do so away from the office. Talk to friends after work or on weekends rather than at the workplace. That way you won't find yourself emotionally raw as you discuss the breakup, only to turn around and have to interact with this man. It's easier to manage your emotions when you draw clear boundaries.

It's also important to set boundaries with your ex. Even if he asks you how you really are, or something like that, keep all your interactions with him professional and clear-cut.

When you're healing from a broken heart, it's important to give yourself time to grieve. Don't let working with this man prevent you from doing that. So go ahead and grieve—just do it away from the office. Over time your pain will ease, and you'll find your sense of freedom at work returning.

—Diane Mandt Langberg, *Today's Christian Woman*, January/February 2000

Q: Thanks to a recent promotion, I'm now making more money than my husband. He feels threatened, as though he's not being a good provider for our family. Any suggestions for navigating this new dynamic in our relationship?

A: It's tempting to equate our value with a concrete measurement like a salary (or weight and age, for that matter). Money is one of the most measurable ways we have of defining our failure or success as a spouse. This is especially true for most husbands.

But our vocation is more than a pathway of provision. It's a response to God's call in our life, an expression of the unique gifts and talents He has given us. If you and your husband have a shared vision of how each of you invest yourselves in your work, as well as a shared ownership of nurturing and providing for your family, then his partnership and support are probably the most valuable provision he could give you as a husband.

Make sure he knows how much his contribution means to you. Affirm how you value his call and his vocational gifts. If he is making sacrifices right now for your career, make clear that you're willing to do the same for him when the time is right. This, as well as true teamwork, will underscore your mutual respect and enable him to redefine his role as provider.

—Leslie Parrott, *Today's Christian Woman*, January/February 2007

Q: During the ten years we have been married, my husband has changed jobs several times, either by quitting or getting fired. He just got fired again last week. He's showing no initiative in looking for a job. I have always been the breadwinner in the family, and I keep trying to support him, but I am losing respect for him. I'm not sure how much longer I can take this.

A: It's understandable that you are weary and losing respect for your husband. He has probably lost a lot of respect for himself.

One way to sort out your feelings is to sit down and write him a letter. In the letter express your love, your hope, and your deepest heart's desire for the possibilities for his life and your marriage. Also clearly communicate your despair, discouragement, and frustration. Put your sense of hopelessness and helplessness into words. Let him know just how serious the situation has become.

If you decide to share your thoughts with your husband, it would be best to give the letter to him and let him process it before discussing it. When you do discuss it, be careful. Use "I" more than "you." Also, watch out for the subtle trap of generalizations such as, "You always" or "You never." The more he senses your disapproval, the more his "failure focus" kicks in and the less motivated he will be.

We encourage you as a couple to join a small group to encourage each other. Seek wise counsel and let your friends help you. Remember not to focus on what you can't change. Dwell on what you with God's help can change.

—Gary J. and Carrie Oliver, *Marriage Partnership*, Spring 2001

Q: I'm pregnant with my first child. I love my job, but I also want to be home with the baby. How can I figure out a way to work and be a stay-at-home mom?

A: Consider the following tips before you're faced with the challenge of balancing financial needs with the needs of your children:

1. *Define what it means to stay at home.* Some full-time moms run a home business after their children go to bed, juggle schedules with their husband, or split their part-time hours between their home and an office. And some fit the traditional picture of a homemaker. What would be ideal for you?

2. *Decide what you value as a couple.* Some husbands are uncomfortable with the thought of being the sole breadwinner.

3. *Live on one income.* Children bring increased expenses, making it difficult to cut back on your lifestyle after they've arrived. Start now by living on one income and saving the earnings of the other.

4. *Visit day-care facilities or check out other options.* First, decide if daycare is something you are comfortable with. If you opt for daycare, visit places that care for infants. Assess whether you'd be comfortable leaving your baby in their care.

5. *Calculate what it costs to work.* Take a moment to calculate the cost of wardrobe, transportation, daycare, lunches out, cleaning services, and whatever else you might spend in the work force. Then calculate the after-tax pay you'll actually bring home.

—Jane A. G. Kise, *Today's Christian Woman*, July/August 2001

How to Launch a Home-Based Business

Pick your profession. Do you bake a positively-out-of-this-world cheese-cake that disappears even before it hits the potluck table? Do friends call you when they can't figure out what their computer is doing? Perhaps you can turn your hobby, skill, or talent into a profitable business. First, take a long look at your skills, hobbies, and interests. If you're willing to let your imagination run wild, the business possibilities are endless.

Work hard. If you go into business for yourself at home, be prepared to work incredibly hard. You'll probably work harder than you ever worked for an employer—for less pay and fewer benefits. If this is your dream, you've prayed about it, and are willing to sacrifice, then keep going.

Create a business plan. A business plan is a written summary of what you would like to do, how much it will cost, and how you plan to do it. If you hope to attract start-up financing from a bank, usually you'll need a written business plan. So once you've decided what product or service you wish to sell, grab some paper and brainstorm answers to the following questions:

What is my business name and slogan? Who are my potential customers? Can they afford this product? Who else is selling the same product or service? What do they charge? How can I make my product or service unique? What do I need to get started? A computer? An industrial sewing machine? A business license?

Take all of these scattered ideas and condense them into a couple of pages.

Your answers will form the basis of your business plan. Contact the Small Business Administration office or your local Chamber of Commerce if you need help writing your plan. There are agencies in almost every community that can help.

Mind your money. As soon as your business plan is complete, see an accountant. Don't wait for tax time to roll around; you may miss important, legitimate business expense deductions. You may be entitled to deduct a percentage of your office space, your heating, and mortgage or rent payment. Check with the IRS for the most current regulations.

Meet with your insurance agent. You don't want to wait for a fire to destroy your business to discover that your regular homeowners policy didn't cover your new color laser printer.

Set up shop. Make a list of your business needs and wants. Then prioritize them. Place a "1" beside those items you absolutely require to begin your business; a "2" next to what you need, but you've got something that will do for now; and a "3" beside those items that would be nice to have some day. You'll need to purchase the necessary items first—and as your business begins to generate money, you can gradually make your way down to your wish list.

Establish business hours. Don't allow distractions, such as the television, to keep you from your work. It's also important to keep your business space off-limits to domestic duties. On the flip side, be aware of your off-work hours. Don't allow your work to interfere with your family, social, and free time. When you shut your door at whatever time you've chosen to end your workday, say good-bye until the following day.

—Linda Hall, *Today's Christian Woman*, September/October 1996

Q: I just got laid off. I'm lost with all of this unexpected time on my hands. What's the best way to navigate this season of unemployment?

A: Here are some positive steps you can take to make the most of this period of change in your life.

1. *Keep a schedule.* Boredom is Enemy No. 1. On Monday mornings, make a list of activities including job hunting, chores, errands, exercise, Bible reading, and hobbies—enough stuff to keep you busy all week. Keep a regular bedtime so you won't be tempted to sleep all day. Also keep the television off during the daytime so you won't be distracted from your "work."

2. While job hunting is a priority, *varying your activities* is essential. Although you may have a lot of bills to pay and no income, spending all of your time job-hunting quickly leads to burnout and depression, which will make your job search more difficult.

3. Keep your spirits lifted by *taking up a (inexpensive) hobby.* Look for low-cost and no-cost ways to have fun. You can find plenty of free entertainment by visiting the library or touring your local historic district.

4. It's important *to find the sense of community* you miss from a job by plugging into more social activities at church, volunteering, or just talking with your friends.

5. Ultimately, though, your greatest comfort comes when you *pray.* As you pour out your needs to God, your perspective may change. You may find yourself thanking God for the solitude of days unfilled by activities as this becomes a time of spiritual renewal.

—Holly Vicente Robaina, *Today's Christian Woman*, July/August 2004

Additional Resources

Books:

The Church in the Workplace: How God's People Can Transform Society,
C. Peter Wagner (Regal, 2006).

Better Than Good: Creating a Life You Can't Wait to Live,
Zig Ziglar (Thomas Nelson, 2007)

Thank You Power: Making the Science of Gratitude Work for You,
Deborah Norville (Thomas Nelson, 2008)

Small Business, Big Life: Five Steps to Creating a Great Life with Your Own Small Business,
Louis Barajes (Thomas Nelson, 2007)

Staying True in a World of Lies: Practical Models of Integrity for Women in the Workplace,
Julie-Alyson Ieron (Christian Publications, 2002)

Websites:

www.RealRelationships.com
Connect with Christian working women

www.faithintheworkplace.com
Real-world issues for Christian working women

www.cwahm.com
Christian Work at Home Moms features encouragement and
resources for mothers who work at home

Questions About

Time
Management

Q: Lately I've been forgetting important family activities, like my daughter's pom-pom performance and my son's football game. I feel bad about disappointing my kids, and I'm starting to resent that I'm the one who has to keep track of every event. How do I stop being the family's social secretary?

A: It's frustrating to miss fun family events and it can be tough to keep everyone's schedules straight. Maybe it's time to enlist your children's help. Brainstorm ideas with them about scheduling. I did this with my kids, and here's the system we came up with:

• Hold a family meeting once a week: Choose a day that works for everyone.

• Ask everyone to share their schedule for the upcoming week. Don't forget to include yourself. Carpooling needs to be a part of the discussion too.

• Purchase Post-It Notes and a mobile planner for organizing. The planner needs to be large enough to include everyone's details (events, phone numbers, locations) yet small enough to be placed in a purse, briefcase, or backpack.

• Create or purchase a family calendar: If you have a computer, set up a family calendar. Help your children type in their events for the entire month. Print and then enlarge the calendar. Put it somewhere visible for everyone to view daily. Another idea is to purchase a Mylar erasable calendar. Give each child a different colored marker to write their weekly and monthly events. The family will learn to identify the specific color for that person. When family members cannot remember where someone is, they can go check it out on the family calendar.

—Barbara Schiller, *Christian Parenting Today*, May/June 2001.

Q: My schedule is always overbooked. How can I train myself to say no when my knee-jerk reaction is to say yes to every request for help and to social events?

A: Whether you're an introvert or an extrovert, trying to please everyone by "doing" only brings about exhaustion or bitterness. And that's certainly not the way God calls us to live. God knows your personality intimately because He made you, and He doesn't expect you to be someone you're not. He also knows you need to stop sometimes and rest.

So figure out how many activities a week you're comfortable with, and then consider those "available slots." Instead of blindly booking activities simply because they arise, make sure you save the slots in your schedule you need for "sanity time."

Some of your stress-inducing situations may be nonnegotiable—such as traveling for your job or keeping up with an energetic toddler. But other activities may be negotiable, such as hosting a wedding shower or chairing a Fun Fair at your child's school. The crucial question is this: Do these negotiable activities stress you out . . . or energize you? If your blood pressure rises when you even *think* about the activity, why not take a pass?

No isn't a dirty word—in fact, sometimes it's one of the healthiest things we can say. After all, sometimes we have to say no—even to good things—in order to say yes to the *best* things. If we're constantly scurrying around like the well-known Martha in Luke 10:38–42, we won't have time to sit, like Mary, at Jesus' feet.

—Ramona Cramer Tucker, *Today's Christian Woman* magazine, September/October 2004

Q: I love being with my friends, but how do I make time for them when my schedule is packed?

A: Hands down, one of the best ways to establish a strong friendship is to make your friend your prayer partner. Praying for one another on a regular basis forms a friendship bond that's deeper than any other. Plus, you're doing double-duty with your time: you're spending quality time together and you're praying.

Doubling up on activities is one of the best ways to build more friend time into your schedule without neglecting your family. For instance, my friend has a daughter the same age as mine. Whenever a movie comes out that the girls would enjoy, we take them. This gives my friend and me time to talk on the drive to the theater, while we munch our popcorn before the movie starts, and then on the drive home. The girls keep each other occupied, and my friend and I have plenty of time together.

When time is limited, it helps to focus your friendships. I know I can maintain regular contact with the six women in my prayer group. Outside of this group are friends that I meet occasionally—say for lunch a few times a year. I make the effort to touch base with them enough so I can maintain our friendship and see how each is doing. While the contact is brief and not as frequent as with close friends, it is still rewarding.

I encourage every woman to take her friendships before the Lord and say, "Lord, show me what I should be doing to honor this friendship and help me find the time to do it."

—Stormie Omartian, Ruth Senter, and Colleen Evans, *Can I Afford Time for Friendships?* (Bethany House, 1994)

Making Time for Friends

Here are some practical ways to make time for the relationships that matter to you:

1. If time is short, look for those activities that allow you to combine time for friends. Be creative. Consider serving on the food committee at church with a friend. As you pack food baskets and deliver them, you'll have time to share in conversation. If you're trying to work exercise into your daily routine, ask a friend to walk with you. It helps the miles go faster when you're talking.

2. If your time with friends seems a little haphazard, then each time you make a contact—phone call, lunch, or walk—make a note of it in your calendar. Then at a glance, you'll know what friends need to be contacted next. And, if you want, even make a note of what's happening in that friend's life so when you do talk again you can remember where your conversation left off.

3. On a piece of paper make four columns. Title the columns: (1) close friends; (2) good friends; (3) casual friends, and (4) budding friendships. Review all of your friendships and place each friend under the appropriate category. Now, look over your list and reflect on how you are spending your time. Are there some names you'd like to see moved from the casual friends to the close friends category? Are you willing to invest more time for that to happen? Use the insights you've gained from this exercise to help you determine where to best use your time.

—Stormie Omartian, Ruth Senter, and Colleen Evans, *Can I Afford Time for Friendships?* (Bethany House, 1994)

Q: For years, I have said yes to so many responsibilities. They all seem important, but somehow they no longer bring me the joy and satisfaction they used to. How can I get off this treadmill and begin enjoying life again?

A: One day, as I rushed through the mall, I caught a glimpse of myself in a mirror. It literally stopped me in my tracks. *Who is that woman with those dark shadows under her eyes?* I knew my life had to change.

To get there, I had to make some hard choices. First, I had a major powwow with my family. After much prayer and planning, I gave up my job and commute. It wasn't an easy decision, and it was a six-month process. We trimmed our finances to the lowest dollar, sold our car, and bought an older model. We aggressively paid off a credit card. I scouted our city for leads on work I could do from home. I still wanted to use the skills I'd developed in my career, but in a different context.

My first month home, I didn't know how to relax. I was a drill sergeant who almost drove my family crazy. I realized I not only needed to pace myself but to find an outlet for the energy I once poured into my work. I began an early-morning exercise program.

Today, I still struggle with time issues, but now I'm juggling only five or six balls instead of twenty. *Simplify. Simplify. Simplify.* Keep saying the words. And until they become second nature, consciously decide to get out of the fast lane and enjoy life again.

—T. Suzanne Eller, *Today's Christian Woman*, July/August 2000

Are You Too Busy?

1. Do you fold socks (or perform any household task) after midnight?
2. Do you skip meals to fulfill responsibilities?
3. Are you ever late because of overlapping responsibilities?
4. Do you travel over the speed limit even when you're not in a hurry?
5. Do you feel torn between family and responsibilities?
6. Do you fall asleep as soon as you sit down?
7. Do you drink coffee/caffeine to stay awake?
8. Do you get sick easily?
9. Do you fight irritability?
10. Do you have difficulty sleeping?
11. Do you lie awake worrying about things you need to do the next day?
12. Do you feel guilty if you do nothing?

INSIGHT

Here's the scoring:

If you answered yes to 4 or more, you're dealing with symptoms of a stressful lifestyle.

If you answered yes to 6 or more, it's time to evaluate family and spiritual priorities.

If you answered yes to 8 or more, take back control of your life.

—T. Suzanne Eller, *Today's Christian Woman*, July/August 2000

Q: I know I should be spending time studying God's Word. For all of my good intentions, I can't seem to make this a consistent part of my life. What are some ways I can find more time for God?

A: Be honest: Is it lack of time, or is something else involved? Many people put Bible study last on their day's agenda then never get to it because they're tired or uninspired. If this is the case, acknowledge the problem.

Sometimes it's easier to develop a habit of Bible reading when you use guides to help you study. Shop around for Bible study books you enjoy. Whether you like a light, personal approach or a more scholarly one, you'll find a wide selection at your local Christian bookstore.

Set aside a specific place and time for Bible study. Human beings are creatures of habit. Find a time when you are energetic and alert, then arrange your schedule accordingly.

Think of your Bible study time as a natural stress reducer. Tell your family you need time alone every day so you can study the Bible.

If you are people-oriented, plan Bible study time with your husband or a friend. Combine this with a workout or a neighborhood stroll before or after study to improve your physical and spiritual health.

Lastly, set priorities. If you get off track, approach Bible study like a diet and get right back on. And, like a diet, with discipline your goal can be reached.

—Denise Turner, *Today's Christian Woman*, March/April 1989

Q: With a husband and family to care for, and a full calendar of activities, how do I make time for me?

A: Personal time for yourself is essential to round out who you are. Without it you end up giving everything you are to everyone else with no time or energy left for you to enjoy life. Here are some ways to make time for yourself:

Learn to delegate. You simply cannot do everything yourself. When you're trying to decide what to delegate, ask yourself, "What can and can't I do well?" Realizing where your weaknesses are will give you some sense for what can be farmed out to others.

Ask questions. This can be an effective means of opening up more time. Pride often stops us from doing this, and we stubbornly insist we can figure it out ourselves. Don't be afraid to ask questions. It'll keep you from doing work yourself, finding out it wasn't right, and then doing it again.

Say goodbye to perfection. Learn to discern when you have spent enough money, time, and/or energy on a project. Do the best you can, then move on.

Develop interests and hobbies. When I take time to visit a museum, or pursue a hobby, it makes me a more interesting person. I have something to share with others that isn't family or work-related. When was the last time you had fun or did something just you enjoyed? If it's been more than a month, block off a morning on your calendar that's just for you. Then keep your eyes open for opportunities to invest that time wisely.

—Judith Briles, Luci Swindoll, and Mary Welchel, *The Workplace: Questions Women Ask* (Bethany House, 1992)

Q: I always have a long list of items on my to-do list. By day's end I feel so discouraged. I've hardly accomplished anything, and I don't know where the time has gone. What can I do to feel more productive?

A: When I looked closer at the flow of a typical day, I realized I operated at a spastic level—writing for thirty minutes, playing computer games for thirty minutes, starting a load of laundry, watching a half hour of television, then writing for another half hour.

When I talked with a friend of mine, she identified with my dilemma. She called it "hummingbird head" syndrome, flitting from one activity to the next but accomplishing little. "It's a lack of focus and it's a huge time killer," she said.

As I talked with other friends, I realized this was a common challenge. Though our schedules and family situations vary greatly and we're in different seasons of life, we all struggle with the issue of time. We identified four culprits that regularly rob us of the valuable moments of our day: Over-commitment, e-mail, TV, and computer games.

To overcome these time stealers, I decided to fast. Instead of giving up food, I eliminated my time stealers for thirty days. I checked my e-mail only twice a day. Computer games were gone. I set limits on the number of programs I watched and refused to turn the television on at all during the day. This forced me to choose a couple of favorite shows, which I watched in the evening with my husband. During the day I popped in a CD and filled my home with my favorite worship music.

As the fast concluded, I looked at what I'd gained. My life hadn't changed, just the management of my time. I still had the same twenty-four hours available to me each day. I still was busy. I still had deadlines. But I'd uncovered pockets of precious moments that I chose to fill carefully. I spent a portion of my morning reading my Bible and talking with God. I took long walks with my husband in the evening or worked outside with our horses. Because my work and tasks for the day were complete, I could enjoy these things with a clear focus and without guilt. Several of these "luxuries" I'd often neglected in the past because I had too much to do and not enough time.

When the fast was over, I came to the conclusion that God had more for me—not a legalistic list of tasks to perform, but a new way of thinking. I began to see the hours of my day as opportunities, each moment as a possibility. Eliminating time stealers has allowed me to concentrate on the things that really matter.

—T. Suzanne Eller, *Today's Christian Woman*, July/August 2003

Q: When my husband and I got married, I imagined we'd always feel the same passion and enthusiasm for our relationship as we did on our wedding day. We used to spend all of our free time together. Now, we're so busy all the time, we rarely enjoy each other's company, and we don't have that same spark between us. What can I do before our marriage fizzles all together?

A: If you are too busy to spend time with your mate, then you are too busy. Here are some tips for making time together to have the kind of marriage you want:

1. *Make one day a week your calendar time.* This is a time when you plan your together times for the week. Set it up like a business or dentist appointment. Plan different types of time, such as fun-only times, dates, or walks to talk about your day or to resolve conflict.

2. *Implement a set of rules to safeguard your time from outside intruders.* Turn off cell phones, pagers, and TVs. If your kids are old enough, talk to them about what Mom and Dad are going to do. Train them on the Three B's rule: Only interrupt if someone is bleeding or broken, or if something is burning.

3. *Be realistic.* There should be a brief "How are you?" connection every day, but as far as carving out twenty to thirty minutes to share your heart, three to four days per week is more realistic.

4. *Don't give up.* Keep working to make it happen. A marathoner has to get over the soreness and get into a routine, but once established, it is easier to keep the training going.

—Dr. Tim A. Gardner, *Marriage Partnership*, Spring 2001

Q: I get together with two friends once a week for girls' night out—usually dinner and a movie. My in-laws think this is strange and make me feel guilty for taking time away from my husband and kids. I think this time is good for me because I always come back recharged and ready to be a mom and wife again. Is this wrong?

A: Making time for friends can be a real struggle. So I'm impressed you've found a way to maintain a solid relationship with your friends. And I like that you mention the "recharge" factor. After days of wiping noses, dinner with friends would be more about getting recharged than about getting a good meal.

Friendships really matter. Scripture shows us how God used friendships to bless people, and this continues today. It's hard to answer your question of "Is this wrong?" Really, you should ask your husband and kids. As long as they feel they get enough of your time and attention during the rest of the week, they're probably happy to have you spend time with friends. And if your night out means a special night of their own with Dad, they probably look forward to it all the more.

On the other hand, if your night out is yet another commitment in your busy life that takes you away from them, they may feel resentful. So ask your husband and kids and, depending on their answer, adjust the frequency of your outings or continue to enjoy.

—Caryn Rivadeneira, "Ask a Resourceful Mom," Christianity Today International, 2006

Q: I get so caught up in the day-to-day tasks of running our home. Most days I end up not having any time for God. How can I develop my prayer life when I'm already short on time to do all the things I need to get done?

A: Sometimes we're so busy putting out fires and dealing with life's little emergencies that we feel like we have no control over our time. But we do. Every woman has to ask herself, "Am I accomplishing the things that are genuinely my priorities, the things that support my value system?"

We need to make appointments with God on our calendars. We have to give those appointments the same weight as the other pressing needs or they aren't going to happen.

The Bible talks about praying without ceasing. If we continually think of every moment of our thought life as unceasing conversation with God, we can always be in prayer. You can pray anywhere, anytime—whether you're giving the kids a bath or paying bills or driving to work.

I encourage women to spend five minutes at the beginning of the day with a short devotional. This will insure you're reading Scripture and it gives you a thought to chew on as you go about your day.

—Carla Barnhill, *Christian Parenting Today*, July/August 2001

Q: Finding the extra minutes in a day to stay healthy seems impossible to me. And even if I had the time to go to the gym between work, dinner, and my kids' soccer practice, where would I begin? I'd never have enough time to get in shape, so why try?

A: If you don't start maintaining the health you've already got, look out, because it doesn't get easier. Investing in your health isn't a luxury. Often women with husbands and kids to care for feel guilty making that investment in themselves. But when you start to lose muscle mass, gain weight, and feel tired all the time, you can't give something you don't have.

It's not easy to get started building fitness time into your schedule. But the first big important step is getting enough sleep. Keeping regular sleeping hours is crucial, because the more disciplined things, such as eating right and exercising, are harder to implement if you're exhausted.

If you sit all day, you'll have to look for opportunities to move around. For example, if you work on the second floor, use the stairs instead of the elevator. Over a period of time, the difference between taking the stairs versus taking the elevator has a significant impact on how much muscle you use and how many calories you burn. Also taking a fifteen-minute walk during your lunch hour or break time can have huge benefits.

Even if you don't have time to do an optimal fitness routine, there's still lots you can do every day to make a huge difference in your health.

—Amy M. Tatum with Ruth McGinnis, *Today's Christian Woman*, September/October 2002

Q: How do I set boundaries so I have time for what's most meaningful to me—my relationships?

A: At one point in my life, I suffered from insomnia for forty-five days straight. When I finally sought the help of a doctor, he told me I had three choices: move to Borneo; take medication, which would only temporarily relieve the symptoms; or radically change my lifestyle. I opted to change my lifestyle.

After my doctor's appointment, I began to study Genesis to see if God had anything to say about my situation. In Genesis 1, I noticed these statements: "And there was evening, and there was morning the first day," and "And there was evening and morning the second day." It does that for the entire creation account.

I realized that the Hebrews followed that account: at 6:00 p.m., they began their day ("And there was evening and morning"). Whatever was first was most important. So for them, the most important part of the day, the relational "season," began at sunset. No rushing, no work. Just a focus on their relationships with God and with others.

I discussed the lifestyle change with my family. We set 6:00 p.m. as the definitive time to be done working for the day. That created a boundary that said we're going to have time for relationships. If something doesn't get finished, it can wait until the next day.

We made the evening meal the first item on our agenda. We have dinner together as a family every night. In our family the meal is a festival.

Everyone jumps in to help: our kids set the table and cut the vegetables, while someone else cooks. Afterwards, we all clean up, do the dishes, and put everything away.

At dinner, we simply ask, "Tell me about your day," and every person gets to share. At the end of the sharing we ask, "How would you rate your day on a scale of 1 to 10?"

Before, I'd spend a little time in the evening with my wife, then I'd go back to work. Because I knew I was going back to work, I was often distracted in the time we were together. Now that I don't go back to work in the evenings, I'm more relaxed, and we have a greater devotion to each other. We have the commitment to spend time together. We've never had that in our life before. But we do now because we created it.

It's changed our priorities. Six to 10:00 p.m. is our destination. When we give ourselves this, we are fulfilling what God intended for us, but we're also making our life balanced, we get better sleep, and we get more work done during the day.

There's a principle that says work takes all the time allotted to it. What we learned is that when you set a deadline for your work, you'll have a greater tendency to get more work done. Couples who don't create boundaries end up letting their work extend into all hours.

—Ginger Kolbaba with Randy Frazee, *Marriage Partnership*, Fall 2005

Q: I've always believed in living an abundant life. Lately, though, I feel burned out. How can I figure out how to spend my time wisely so I can get my sanity back?

A: Several years ago I felt the same way. I had a full life—a good marriage, a child, a career. Somewhere along the way, I started feeling as though I were living someone else's life. I couldn't seem to measure up to the expectations I had placed on my life. As I sorted out my thoughts, I realized there were truths about living an abundant life I'd totally misunderstood. Here is what I learned:

1. *You have to run your own race.* Our culture constantly evaluates whether we're successful by measuring everything from our bank account to our IQ to how many miles we can run without full cardiac arrest. The benchmark isn't how well we do, but how well we do compared to everyone else. So whenever I used to read Hebrews 12:1, "Let us run with perseverance the race marked out for us," I'd picture myself running alongside my sisters in Christ, constantly trying to gauge how I was doing. "Was I spiritual enough?" Then I revisited Hebrews 12:1, and the Holy Spirit illuminated something I'd been missing: We're to run the race marked out for *us*.

2. *You can't do it all.* The truth is, we can't do it all. Acknowledging our limitations means letting go of an unrealistic ideal, setting boundaries, saying no more often, and prioritizing what's left. God doesn't expect us to do it all.

—Verla Gillmor, *Today's Christian Woman*, July/August 2002

Additional Resources

Books:

Thrilled to Death: How the Endless Pursuit of Pleasure Is Leaving Us Numb,
Dr. Archibald Hart (Thomas Nelson, 2008)

Breathing Freely: Celebrating the Imperfect Life,
Ruth McGinnis (Revell, 2002)

Making Room for Life: Trading Chaotic Lifestyles for Connected Relationships,
Randy Frazee (Zondervan, 2004)

Sacred Sex: A Spiritual Celebration of Oneness in Marriage,
Dr. Tim A. Gardner and Scott M. Stanley (WaterBrook, 2002)

Reality Check: A Survival Manual for Christians in the Workplace,
Verla Gillmor (Horizon Books, 2001)

Websites:

www.timeoutforwomen.com
Website for Time Out for Women conferences

www.lifechasers.org
A ministry resource for Christians who work

Magazines:

Today's Christian Woman.
Timely, practical insights into all aspects of a woman's life

Marriage Partnership.
Quarterly publication that provides practical,
thoughtful articles on all aspects of the married life

Questions
About

Money
& Finances

Q: I often think that if I just had a little more money, I'd be happier and so many of my problems would go away. Is this true?

A: People tend to believe four common myths about money:

Myth 1: *Money equals happiness.* Who knows for sure that money doesn't bring happiness? Only people with loads of money. If your life outside the financial realm doesn't bring you more satisfaction than the idea of big bucks, you need to realign your thinking.

Myth 2: *Money equals importance.* God has proved you are worth the very life of His Son. The value we find in our material possessions is enormously wimpy compared to the sacrifice Christ made for us. Need a designer label? It's time for a worth check.

Myth 3: *Money equals fulfillment.* It's not wrong to have nice things for yourself or your family. But it's wrong to love nice things so much that we go into debt for them and give them too much importance. We should aim for balance and a godly perspective.

Myth 4: *We own our possessions.* We don't own anything, not even ourselves. God's Word says we were bought at a price, and we are not our own (1 Cor. 6:19–20). The secret to being content with what we have is recognizing God's ownership and giving Him control. When we give Him control and recognize that everything belongs to Him, we're set free from stewing over money.

—Rhonda Rhea, *Today's Christian Woman*, January/February 2003

Q: I'm caught in a cycle of overspending. Why is handling money so difficult for me?

A: According to a recent CNBC survey, 43 percent of American families spend more than they earn. The average household carries more than $8,000 in consumer debt. Understanding what purpose spending serves for us as women can go a long way toward breaking our spending cycle.

For example, when we spend without a specific need in mind, we frequently overspend. We may not wrestle with impulse buying when we stop at the grocery store for items on a list, but when it comes to shopping for food to bring to a party, emotions color our buying.

If we want to make a U-turn from the addictions of affluence, we can reverse our course with these steps.

1. *Start with small changes.* Don't roll back spending in every area. Begin with one or two problem spots.

2. *Determine your financial priorities.* Figure out your family goals: how you'll spend your money, what kind of debt (if any) you feel comfortable with that won't endanger your family's financial health, how much you'll save. Keep these goals in mind as you make spending decisions.

3. *Give away more.* Giving reverses materialistic impulses and allows us to focus on others rather than ourselves. Can you increase your giving within the limits of your income? If so, give in ways that reflect your values.

—Donna Savage, *Today's Christian Woman*, November/December 2006

Q: How can a woman establish credit?

A: First, get a secured credit card from your bank by putting down a deposit. Every month charge a small amount such as $25, then pay that off. Once you have a credit history established, you can move to an unsecured card that doesn't require a deposit.

Then, get two or three cards, charge small amounts, and pay them off every month so you can establish a positive payment pattern on your credit report.

—Deborah McNaughton, *Today's Christian Woman*, September/October 2000

Q: Is it okay to have several credit cards?

A: It's better to have two credit cards, but not a department store or gas card, because those cards have very high interest. Get a Visa or a Master-Card with a low interest rate. Just make sure when you get the cards, you read the fine print on their disclosures so you'll know how much and when interest is charged. Some interest is charged the minute you make a purchase, while others have a grace period of maybe twenty-five days.

All the cards you have—whether you use them or not—are listed on your credit report. When someone checks your credit, these cards will appear as if they're active accounts, even if you haven't used them for years. That means technically you can run up those credit limits.

If you're not using credit cards, it's a good idea to close the accounts. Cut the cards up and return them to the creditor. If you don't have the cards, write a letter. Send it certified mail and tell them you want the account closed. Then follow up within four to six weeks to make sure the creditor reports that the consumer closed the account. Don't just trust they'll close it. Follow up on it. If the account looks as if it's open, it'll stay on your credit report forever. If it shows you've closed it, then that account stays on your report for seven years. A bankruptcy stays listed for ten years.

—Deborah McNaughton, *Today's Christian Woman,* September/October 2000

Q: How can I check my credit rating?

A: You should get a copy of your credit report at least once a year from the three credit reporting agencies: Experian, Trans Union, and Equifax (see page 93). That way, you can make sure everything is as it should be. You need to get a report from each agency because you don't know which reporting agency a creditor will use.

Once you get a copy of your report, go through every entry and make sure it's reported accurately. If it's not, write a letter pointing out the inaccuracy to that credit agency. If the error is on all three credit reports, you must write all three agencies separately. One letter won't fix all.

Reporting agencies have to complete their investigation within thirty days and send you a report. So if the report says your account has gone to a collection agency and you know you've paid the bill, send a letter of dispute. The agency will send the dispute letter to the creditor. If the creditor doesn't respond within a reasonable time period—about twenty-one days—it will come off the report automatically. Then the reporting agency has to send you an updated report showing what happened. You cannot take creditors at their word. You must get it in writing.

—Deborah McNaughton, *Today's Christian Woman*, September/October 2000

Where to Get a Credit Report

If you have been denied credit based on information in one
of these reports, you're entitled to a free copy of your credit report under
the federal Fair Credit Reporting Act. Put in your request within
sixty days of your denial, however.

Even if you haven't been denied credit, it's a good idea to review
your credit reports periodically to make sure the information listed
is correct. Typically, each report costs $8. If there are errors, straighten them
out now—before you apply for a mortgage or car loan.

Equifax 1-800-685-1111 / **www.equifax.com**

Experian 1-888-397-3742 / **www.experian.com**

Trans Union 1-800-888-4213 / **www.transunion.com**

—Deborah McNaughton, *Today's Christian Woman*, September/October 2000.

Q: I'm a married woman. Should I establish my own credit even if my husband handles the finances?

A: A married woman should always get credit in her own name. You may think you have credit because you're the one who writes the checks, or you have a joint account with your husband, or you use a credit card that has your husband's name on it and you're authorized to use it. But if something happens to your husband and you try to buy something on credit, it will come up as "No record found." You thought you had credit, but you didn't.

Also if there's ever a financial problem with your husband's credit or your joint accounts, keeping your card in good standing may help you reestablish your credit.

If your husband handles the finances, sit down with him every month and go over all the bills. And get copies of your credit report—that will tell you how the bills are being paid, especially if they're joint. Women need to make sure they're aware of what's happening with their finances.

—Deborah McNaughton, *Today's Christian Woman*, September/October 2000

Q: How can I protect myself financially if divorce is imminent?

A: Divorce can be a financial mess for women. As soon as the divorce proceedings start, make sure you close every joint credit account. If your husband wants to keep it open, you have to insist, and send a letter to all your creditors, stating you're in the process of a divorce and you want your name removed from the account. If you don't and the judge rules your husband has to make payments, but he quits, that will affect your credit.

Another way to make sure you're protected is to find out if your husband is behind on any taxes, because that can spill over onto you even after the divorce is final.

—Deborah McNaughton, Today's Christian Woman, September/October 2000

FINANCES

MONEY &

Q: I just discovered that my husband has racked up enormous credit-card debt on top of our large student loans. I had always assumed there were no financial secrets between us, but apparently I was wrong. What can I do?

A: You and your husband need help. Set an appointment with a financial consultant. Ask for advice on how to handle your current debt and how to keep from accruing more.

I also suggest marriage counseling. Your husband's integrity is questionable, and your trust in him has been profoundly shaken. Your marriage is at risk for greater damage. Marriage counseling can help you both understand what's behind your husband's overspending (he may need some individual counseling) and help you repair the damage already done to your relationship.

It's possible your husband will refuse both of these suggestions or simply assure you that he'll stop spending and everything will be fine. Don't settle for that response. It's highly improbable your husband will stop without help. See a counselor on your own if he refuses to join you.

If your husband persists in his behavior and rejects help after you've consulted with a financial adviser and counselor, talk to a lawyer to see if there's some way you can protect yourself from mounting debt. You also may want to bring in a pastor or church leader to help you confront your husband with his destructive behavior. Share your struggle with a few trusted friends so they will understand what you're facing and pray for you as you struggle with this difficult issue.

—Diane Mandt Langberg, *Today's Christian Woman*, May/June 2002

Q: Should I tithe if it will put my family in the situation of needing a miracle to make it through the rest of the month, or should we get our debt under control and then tithe?

A: A tithe is a tenth of your income, which is a biblical mandate that the Christian church has taken to heart (Deut. 26:1–19). But there's no place in Scripture where it says that failing to tithe will send you to hell.

The question is, what's the best thing to do and why does God ask us to tithe? Is it because He needs our money? No. He tells us to tithe because of what giving does inside us. It keeps us from being so stinking self-centered that we think the world revolves around us. And by being a little less self-centered, we're better humans. We're a little more Christ-like when we give—even though God doesn't need our money.

Should you tithe on your income if you need a miracle to get through the rest of the month? Honestly, if you can't live on 90 percent, it's unlikely that you can live on 100 percent.

If you sit down and do a monthly budget, you can probably find a way to tithe if it's important to you. Pray and read the Bible and let God speak to you on this. But this point is clear: The Bible doesn't say wait until you get your debt under control; it says tithe before spending money on anything else.

—Dave Ramsey, *Today's Christian*, January/February 2006

Q: What advantage is there to buying a home versus renting?

A: The financial benefits of owning your residence versus renting are so extensive that I almost always recommend that the purchase of a home be a couple's top investment priority.

First, there are tax advantages to owning your home. The interest portion of your loan payments is generally tax-deductible, meaning that after tax savings are considered, you can afford a substantially larger mortgage payment than rent payment. For example, if you are in a 30 percent federal tax bracket, a $1,000 mortgage payment will cost about the same after taxes as a $700 rent payment. Conversely, a mortgage payment will cost you less on an after-tax basis than a rent payment of an identical amount.

Second, owning your residence increases your net worth. The gap between your home's value and your loan balance is called "equity." This gap grows and your equity builds as your home appreciates in value and as your loan balance declines with each monthly payment.

Third, your mortgage payments remain stable for the term of the loan, while rent payments can increase each year.

The benefits of home ownership extend well beyond the numbers. The extra responsibilities of a home tend to mature us. Owning a home gives one a sense of pride that renting does not yield. Do your homework, and your home-buying experience can be a richly rewarding experience, both personally and financially.

—Scott Kays, *Marriage Partnership*, Spring 2001

Q: I'm facing a financial crisis. How can I weather this storm?

A: When facing a financial crisis, *stay calm.* This will help you think logically.

Next, *quit spending money.* When faced with a financial challenge, it's easy to use your credit cards. But you may run up your balance to the credit limit and not be able to afford the payments, which will result in a poor credit rating—something you won't want during a crisis time.

Now, *prioritize your bills.* Pay essential, or survival, bills first: food, mortgage or rent, utilities. Then, pay car insurance, medical necessities, child support, and any loans such as automobiles and furniture that are secured as collateral. Then pay the nonessential bills—those debts in which no immediate consequences occur if paid late: credit and charge cards, attorney, medical, and accounting bills, newspaper and magazine subscriptions, life insurance, childcare, gyms, or clothing.

Now, *consider negotiating with creditors.* If you can't pay your bills or can only pay a partial amount, your creditors may be able to help you to establish a repayment plan. Some lenders will allow you to defer one payment a year, meaning the payment for that particular month doesn't have to be made. The deferred payment is added to the end of the contract.

Take notes of any conversations with creditors, listing the date and person with whom you spoke. Whatever arrangement you make, get it in writing from the creditor before you send in money.

—Deborah McNaughton, *Marriage Partnership,* Winter 2002

Q: If your finances are a mess, when should you consider filing bankruptcy?

A: Filing for bankruptcy is almost never a good idea. I tell people to file for bankruptcy about as often as I tell them to file for divorce—I don't. There are always situations where good people get into bad situations, but I think many divorces are the result of people giving up too soon. Most bankruptcies are hasty reactions, too.

People who consider bankruptcy are overwhelmed. You need to draw back from your situation and not be emotional. Consider selling your car, taking an extra job, living on a budget, and having a garage sale. Those are all steps that will help you chip away at debt. Then, take care of necessities such as food, shelter, clothing, transportation, and utilities. You may take a few dings on your credit along the way, but you can still map out a plan where you not only get caught up but become completely debt-free in about two years.

You should never file bankruptcy on something you can clean up in two years. Never!

—Dave Ramsey, *Today's Christian*, March/April 2006

Q: How do I know when I can retire?

A: To determine how much to save to prepare for this phase of your life, first determine your retirement income needs. There is no right or wrong answer here, but, assuming your house is paid for, a good rule-of-thumb is that you will require about 70 percent of your pre-retirement annual income to maintain your lifestyle.

A financial planner can calculate the amount you need to save each month to reach your retirement income goals. But here are the general guidelines: If you are in your late 20s or early 30s and are just starting to save for retirement, you should set aside about 10 percent of your monthly gross income. If you are in your late 30s or early 40s, you need to bump that figure up to approximately 15 percent of your income. Ratchet it up to 20 percent if you are in your late 40s or early 50s and just getting started.

Finally, if you are one of the unfortunate ones who are older than that and are just now accumulating assets for retirement, it is unlikely you will be able to save enough to become financially independent by age sixty-five. Extending your career a few years may be necessary to secure an adequate retirement income.

—Scott Kays, *Marriage Partnership*, Winter 2000

Eleven Ways to Cut Holiday Spending

Some tips to help you enjoy the Christmas season without getting into debt:

1. *Now you're cookin'.* People are constantly looking for new dishes to put on their table. Why not compile the recipes you're famous for into one cookbook? For an extra treat, add a jar of homemade salsa or jam or cookie mix to inspire the future cook.

2. *Cherished moments.* Last Christmas, my friend Vikki received a Memory Jar from her friend Dawn just before Dawn moved out of state. On pieces of paper Dawn wrote her favorite memories the friends had shared and put them in a decorative jar. Now, even though they're apart, Vikki and Dawn keep filling the jar by adding things they continue to remember or new memories they make on trips to visit each other.

3. *Double up.* Order double prints when developing film. When I leaf through my pictures at the drug store, I mentally decide who gets the second print of my favorite snaps. I recently came across a great picture of my mom and me. While still at the drugstore, I found a frame for it. Instantly, I had the perfect Christmas gift for my hard-to-buy-for mom.

4. *Coupon craze.* My friend Tokoshi is a genius at flower arranging. As a gift to me, she printed coupons redeemable for floral arranging lessons taught by her. She put the coupons in a bag with floral scissors and a list of other items I needed to bring to "school." Whether your coupons are to teach your niece to bake or your mom to scuba dive, you'll be giving two gifts in one: the lessons and your time.

5. *This is your life.* When my friend Linda turned age fifty, her best friend gave her the issue of *Life* magazine from the week she was born. This inexpensive gift that she had scooped up at an antique store was the hit of the party.

6. *Letter brigade.* My friend Bill wanted to give his wife, Patti, something special while staying within their newlywed budget. On the sly, Bill contacted Patti's closest friends and relatives and asked them to write letters to her about why she is special to them. Bill had the letters mailed to his office, then wrapped them up to give Patti on Christmas.

7. *Reading room.* For your child's teacher, try an age-appropriate book signed by your child to add to the in-class library.

8. *Subscribe today.* Do you have a budding shutterbug in the family? Show your support for your child's passion by giving him or her a subscription to a photography magazine. Buy the current issue off the newsstand and wrap it up with a few rolls of film.

9. *Custom costuming.* Stretch your children's imaginations. Decorate a box to hold cast-off uniforms, jewelry, hats, and shoes to create a treasure chest of dress-up clothes.

10. *Play it again.* Make a recording of yourself reading your child's favorite book so he can hear it over and over. This gift will be appreciated by your child as well as the baby sitter.

11. *Family field trip.* Give a family membership to a local museum or zoo. Be sure to find out what special events and benefits exist for members: a special newsletter for kids, members-only hours, discounts on programs and special deals at the gift shop.

—Kathi Hunter, *Today's Christian Woman*, November/December 2002

Q: What are some financial lessons we should be teaching our children?

A: Kids have no concept that a check or an ATM card represents money. So when you go to an ATM and make a deposit, write a check or withdraw money, explain to them what happens.

Our kids will follow our example. How do you spend your money? What's your attitude toward credit? Children will pick up on that. But you also need to talk to them about finances—especially credit—because no one else will. The schools don't teach them about money; the church doesn't teach them about money. If they don't understand how to properly handle a credit card, then when they turn eighteen and have all these vendors sending them cards, they'll start charging everything they can without realizing how to repay it.

Sit down with your kids and explain the credit system: "You just ran up $2,000 worth of charges? Well, $2,000 is no big deal. You'll only have to make a $20 monthly payment (or whatever the minimum payment is). But let's calculate that out." Then show them that it will take more than sixteen years to pay that off—plus they'll pay $2,500 in interest.

—Deborah McNaughton, *Today's Christian Woman*, September/October 2000

Additional Resources

Books:

The Total Money Makeover: A Proven Plan for Financial Fitness,
Dave Ramsey (Thomas Nelson, 2007)

The 25-Day Money Makeover for Women,
Francine L. Huff (Revell, 2007)

How to Save Money Every Day,
Ellie Kay (Revell, 2004)

*A Christian's Guide to Investing: Managing Your Money, Planning for the Future,
and Leaving a Legacy,* Danny Fontana (Revell, 2005)

*Women, Get Answers About Your Money: Because There Are No Dumb Questions
About Personal Finance,* Carolyn Castleberry (Multnomah, 2006)

Rich in Every Way: Everything God Says About Money and Possessions,
Gene A. Getz (Howard Books, 2004).

God and Your Stuff: The Vital Link Between Your Possessions and Your Soul,
Wesley K. Willmer and Martyn Smith (NavPress, 2002).

Websites:

www.financialvictory.com Financial Victory Institute specializes in credit and financial
education. It provides valuable financial advice directly to consumers

www.elliekay.com Helps women around the world gain control of their money and
find new meaning in life by expanding their roles in their communities

www.soundmindinvesting.com Financial online newsletter
written from a biblical perspective

www.daveramsey.com Advice for getting out of debt
and obtaining financial peace of mind

Questions About **Home** **& Hospitality**

Q: I suffer from agoraphobia. I feel paralyzed at the prospect of having company into my home and worse at the thought of going to someone else's house. What should my perspective on hospitality be as I try to take small steps to overcome this debilitating fear?

A: I used to suffer from anxiety disorder, which included agoraphobia. I'm grateful that when life started coming together for me, I was able to begin extending hospitality. But it took a long time for me to open my home to others because I thought everything had to look the way it did in books or in other people's homes.

Unfortunately, when we think of hospitality, usually it's in narrow terms. We think of someone who can cook or decorate like Martha Stewart. But true hospitality isn't limited to the home. Think about a time when someone showed you she cared that you were struggling and reached out, or someone spent time with you when you were hurting. Or perhaps an absolute stranger extended an unexpected courtesy in the middle of an abrupt world that couldn't care less. That's true hospitality—kindness that makes you feel special, loved, cared for, heard.

Every day we have the chance to make some kind of investment in the lives of everyone with whom we come in contact. I like to think of hospitality as being "hospital-able"—able to be tenderhearted, gracious, and helpful to the wounded, lonely people in the world today. Whether it's in an airport, a hotel lobby, or an arena, I have the opportunity to extend God's love to the people I encounter.

—Patsy Clairmont with Jane Johnson Struck, *Today's Christian Woman*, September/October 1998

Q: I'm not the tidiest person in the world. Now that I'm married, I realize the effect my lax habits are having on my husband. Do you have any tips on how to keep my house looking neater on a regular basis?

A: Here are some systems that help me keep my house clean most of the time, even with the addition of a young child. I decided what fast, simple, daily cleanups would get the house into acceptable shape and keep it there. They had to require no more than a total of thirty minutes. Here's what that consists of in my house:

1. Give the bathroom(s) a two-to-three-minute going-over. This should include wiping off major surfaces from the least germy (top of vanity) to most (back and around bottom of toilet), and picking up towels. If you have a kids' bathroom, get them to clean their own.

2. Vacuum the kitchen, bathroom, living-room rug, rugs in the child's bedroom, and under the dining-room table. I keep the vacuum in the front closet so it's always handy.

3. Spray and wipe the kitchen floor with a dust mop. After I've given the kitchen floor a quick once-over, the mop is just damp enough to act as a dust mop for the hardwood floors in the living room, dining room, and bedrooms.

These tasks, along with whatever kitchen cleanup needs doing, keep my house looking presentable. The beauty of having this bare minimum list and *sticking to* it is that when disaster hits, such as sickness or a major crisis, you can keep the house from deteriorating past a certain level.

—Deborah Simons, *Today's Christian Woman*, January/February 2006

Q: I do a pretty good job of keeping up with the daily housekeeping chores. But how can I move beyond the surface and get deep cleaning done?

A: If you keep your house relatively tidy daily, you're set to tackle the actual cleaning. There are four basic systems, with any number of possible variations:

1. *Clean by the clock.* Decide on the amount of time you have for cleaning and set a timer. When the timer chimes, you're done. Tomorrow you pick up where you left off.

2. *Clean by the room.* Monday is kitchen day, Tuesday is bathroom day and so on. This method has the advantage of getting one entire area done at once.

3. *Clean by the job.* One day may be all the vacuuming and dusting, another all the floor scrubbing. This system has the advantage of requiring only one type of cleaning supplies at a time.

4. *Clean the whole house at once.* This method is for those who have lots of energy or lots of helpers.

5. *Schedule the odd jobs.* These are the tasks that only need to be done monthly or quarterly. Vacuuming the refrigerator coils is a monthly job. Washing the windows is an annual or semi-annual task. Set your standards, then figure out a way to remind yourself to get them done.

Two final principles: When everything around you is in chaos, just step in and do something. And when you're about to drop with exhaustion, stop. Remember Scarlett O'Hara's famous words in *Gone With the Wind*: "Tomorrow is another day." The dust bunnies will still be there.

—Deborah Simons, *Today's Christian Woman*, January/February 2006

Q: I do very little entertaining because I work full time. Is there any way to make my work place more hospitable?

A: The principles of being hospitable—reaching out to others in need, creating a haven for others to enjoy—also translates at work. Here's how you can make your workplace a little warmer:

1. Pray that the peace and presence of Christ is noticeable in your work-space so that when people step into your cubicle or office, they're aware of a difference.

2. Keep note cards in your desk. When you see someone in your workplace having a down day, write her a little note: "I can see that you're struggling, and I want you to know I'm cheering you on."

3. Make your desk more inviting. Fill a small vase with a few fresh flowers you cut from your garden every few days. A neat, organized workspace with sweet, winsome touches draws people in.

—Patsy Clairmont with Jane Johnson Struck, *Today's Christian Woman*, September/October 1998

Q: I have a hard time getting my three children to help me with household chores. They whine, they moan, they procrastinate. I work full time and need their cooperation around the house, but I'm out of creative ideas to motivate them. What can I do?

A: Try this: Make a list of what you consider privileges—television, Instant Messenger, time with friends, computer time, etc.—and explain to your kids that in the real world, you work before you rest, earn before you spend, and pay before you play.

Since one of your jobs is to train them to be successful adults, you're doing them a disservice by letting them enjoy a free ride. They need to earn their room, board, and bonuses by working around the house.

Think of all the household duties, and divide them up between the three children. They can vacuum, load the dishwasher, and even do the laundry. Make a daily chart of responsibilities and post it in a prominent spot.

Make all privileges contingent on completed chores. Sure, they may shirk their responsibilities and say, "I don't care; I don't want to watch TV anyway." But believe me, there will come a day when they desperately want to go to a friend's house, or absolutely have to check their e-mail, or need to watch a TV program. That's when you calmly ask, "Are your chores done?" Stick to your guns. You'll probably have to prove you mean business a few times, so don't cave in.

—Lisa Welchel, *Today's Christian Woman*, May/June 2005

Q: My parents love our kids, and they often offer to baby-sit. Only problem is they let safety rules slide when they're in charge of our kids. What can I do?

A: While it's wonderful when you can look to your own family for childcare, that sweet arrangement can turn sour if you and your parents (or in-laws) don't see eye-to-eye on safety. Often, all it takes to help your parents and in-laws be more safety-conscious is a gentle reminder of what you'd like them to do.

Before you drop your children off at their grandparents' house (or anyone else's, for that matter), it's a good idea to do a quick sweep of the house or the room where they'll be playing. If you see something that bothers you, politely ask if you can fix it or put it in a safer place.

Keep in mind that when grandparents don't see your family on a regular basis, they may not be prepared for the changes in your child. If your baby wasn't even crawling the last time you visited Grandma, she might not be aware of just how active your now-walking toddler can be. If you're planning a visit, call ahead and talk about ways the grandparents can prepare their home for your children. Offer to bring baby gates, outlet plugs, or whatever you'll need to make their home safer.

As parents, keeping our children safe is one of our most important jobs. And while it can be awkward to advise our own parents on childrearing issues, doing so with respect can go a long way toward making sure our children are safe, even when they're away from us.

—Rachelle Vander Schaaf, *Christian Parenting Today*, July/August 2000

Peace Talks About Child Safety

When differences about safety surface with your child's grandparents, do your best to avoid a full-blown argument. Instead of getting angry, try one of these responses:

IF THEY SAY:

"We've always kept cleaning supplies under the sink, even when you were small. Why move them now?"

> **YOU CAN:**
> Appeal to their pride, saying something like, "Jake likes to imitate people he loves, especially you. If he sees you spraying something, he might be tempted to pull out the can and do the same. I'm worried he might aim it into his own eyes."

> **IF THEY SAY:**
> "All that safety gear takes the fun out of going to the park. She's only on training wheels, and it's such a short ride. Why bother with all this stuff?"

YOU CAN:

State the facts. "Did you know that a kid who wears a helmet is 85 percent less likely to suffer a head injury if she falls? Plus, if she gets into the habit of wearing her helmet now, she'll be more likely to keep wearing one when she's older and can ride on the street. I'm sure you, like me, really want her to be protected then."

IF THEY SAY:

"Do we really have to keep him in that car seat in the back? Andy looks so confined there. It'd be much nicer to have him sitting up front."

YOU CAN:

Remind them of the law. "The law says all kids under age four must sit in safety seats. Andy has been riding in a car seat since he was born; he's used to it, and he gets a better view out the window. He should never sit up front because your car has an air bag on the passenger side. If it opens, even during a fender bender, it could hurt or even kill him. Even if there's no air bag, kids are much safer in the back seat."

IF THEY SAY:

"All those locks and latches are expensive and complicated. I don't think they're worth the money and trouble."

YOU CAN:

Be generous. "You're right, it all adds up, and some of those locks are a little tricky. They have to be because kids are masters at getting into trouble. I'll pick up everything we need and put it in place. If something seems complicated, we can figure it out together."

IF THEY SAY:

"Parents today rely on all these gadgets so they don't have to pay attention to the kids. When you were little, we watched you and made sure you didn't get into trouble."

YOU CAN:

Reassure them: "We do our best to make sure Sara stays safe and knows her limits. But there have been a lot of new discoveries about kids and safety in the last thirty years that we think help keep our children even safer. We'd rather be overly cautious than risk an unnecessary accident."

—Rachelle Vander Schaaf, *Christian Parenting Today*, July/August 2000

Q: We recently bought a new house. I've heard of people having their homes blessed. What is this exactly, and how do you do it?

A: Many Christian faiths, such as the Episcopal Church, have used the house blessing for centuries. But while these formal house blessings are typically performed by a priest, anyone can invite God to be part of a family dwelling. To plan your own house blessing, consider these ideas for a stress-free, fun-filled, do-it-yourself ceremony:

1. Plan the event as a family. Several days before your house blessing, sit down with your children and discuss the ingredients of this special event. Will it include music? Will the decorations be homemade?

2. If your house is truly new, try to do a house blessing before the dry-wall is painted. Then, have every member of the family use pencils to write "Dear God" letters describing their hopes and dreams for life in this house on the walls in each room. Even after the paint and paper go up, your kids will remember that their messages to God will always be part of their house.

3. Don't just have a token prayer in the entryway. Plan on winding your way through all the rooms in the house as a way of presenting the whole dwelling to the Lord. Have each family member choose a room for which they'd like to pray.

—Greg Asimakoupoulos, *Christian Parenting Today*, Fall 2003

Prayers for a House Warming

Use some of the following Bible verses during your house blessing:

• Unless the LORD builds the house, its builders labor in vain. (Ps. 127:1 NIV)

• By wisdom a house is built, and through understanding it is established; through knowledge its rooms are filled with rare and beautiful treasures. (Prov. 24:3–4 NIV)

• The LORD bless you and keep you; the LORD make his face shine upon you and be gracious to you; the LORD turn his face toward you and give you peace. (Num. 6:24–26 NIV)

• Do not forget to entertain strangers, for by so doing some people have entertained angels without knowing it. (Heb. 13:2 NIV)

• God said, "Now my eyes will be open and my ears attentive to the prayers offered in this place. I have chosen and consecrated this temple so that my Name may be there forever. My eyes and my heart will always be there." (2 Chron. 7:15–16 NIV)

• Do not store up for yourselves treasures on earth, where moth and rust destroy, and where thieves break in and steal. But store up for yourselves treasures in heaven, where moth and rust do not destroy, and where thieves do not break in and steal. For where your treasure is, there your heart will be also. (Matt. 6:19–21 NIV)

—Greg Asimakoupoulos, *Christian Parenting Today*, Fall 2003

INSIGHT

Q: Are there ways I can decorate for the holidays without breaking the bank or losing the focus of the Christmas season?

A: Yes, there are definitely some simple, sophisticated things you can do to make your house look festive. I tend to decorate my dining room table for the holidays first. Make a dramatic table arrangement by blending roses, hydrangeas, and golden pomegranates. I love to use eucalyptus leaves with sprigs of lavender and poppy pods. You can make them into a long-lasting swag on a mantel or dining room table.

My fireplace mantel is also a favorite focal point. Instead of using the typical evergreen swag, try a magnolia garland, or even pulling holly sprigs from a tree in your yard and adding pears or pomegranates.

When it comes to decorating, I have a "less is more" philosophy. I like to place a simple green garland adorned with tiny white lights around the doorways inside. We use the same white lights outside, too. We'll string the lights on the balustrade of our big white porch and put a pretty wreath on the door.

Keeping it simple doesn't mean your home loses the warmth of family at Christmas. The smells of Christmas—from greenery to baking—can transform your home during the holidays.

For holiday decorating, throw pillows can be an easy way to brighten a room, especially if you sew. I know many women who keep a neutral color palette in their living room, and they're able to rotate in seasonal throw pillows.

—Melissa Hambrick with *Trading Spaces* interior designer Laurie Smith,
Today's Christian Woman, November/December 2003

Q: At Christmas I always end up feeling like commercialism robs us of the true meaning. What are some ways to keep the focus on Jesus?

A: Consider incorporating new traditions into your celebration. Here are some fresh ideas for the holidays:

1. *Think thankfulness.* Find a beautiful blank journal, or create one with handmade papers, and write the year's blessings in it. This can be a private exercise or a family tradition.

2. *Give joy to the world.* Share the Christmas message with everyone who visits your home. Cut gold or silver shimmer fabric into squares. Place several wrapped candies and a copy of a holiday verse such as Isaiah 9:6, Luke 2:11, or Matthew 1:21 inside. Then tie the squares up with sparkly ribbon. Keep a basket of these favors by your front door to bestow on visitors.

3. *Give Jesus a gift.* Offer Jesus a symbolic gift in honor of His birthday. Give Him an area of your life you desire to change—an emotion, an activity, or a relationship—and physically wrap a box to represent it. Do this individually or as a family.

4. *Enjoy simple pleasures.* Set aside an annual night to relish simple, old-fashioned joys. Pop some corn and snuggle with a book of sentimental Christmas stories. If you have kids, plan a night of games and pizza. Saunter through the snow-covered woods or, if you live in a warmer climate, grab a blanket, head outside, and search for the star in the East.

—Jeanne Winters, *Today's Christian Woman*, November/December 2006

HOSPITALITY

119

HOME &

Q: I am knee-deep in motherhood, elbow-deep in laundry, and struggling to fit our family supper into my daily to-do list. Can you suggest some creative ways I can handle the meal planning and cooking for my family?

A: I had the exact same problem: I was too busy to cook. Then a friend invited me to help coordinate a supper-swapping club with her and two other families in our area. Here's how it works:

Dinner is delivered to my door Monday through Wednesday. My cooking day is Thursday. So on Wednesday evening after my kids go to bed, I prepare and assemble four identical meals, such as baked spaghetti and garlic bread, and stack them in my fridge. On Thursday I deliver my three meals to my supper-swapping girlfriends. For about one to two hours of meal preparation and clean-up time and thirty minutes of delivery, I have a week's worth of homemade meals for my family.

We currently have four families in our supper-swapping club (also called a cooking co-op). Some clubs operate with five families, covering the entire workweek. Some operate with three, and eat leftovers the other two nights. Some choose to meet Sunday evening in one location and exchange all of their meals for the week. It's up to you!

Here's how to start a cooking co-op:

1. *Set a trial period.* Ask everyone to commit for a specific amount of time to give supper swapping a fair shake. We began ours with a three-month trial period and gave everyone the option of bowing out after that time. Try to pick families around the same size as yours and with similar tastes and lifestyles.

2. *Define a meal.* We only prepare and deliver two dishes: a main dish and a side or dessert. Other clubs choose to include a complete meal. Be upfront about food likes, dislikes, and allergies. We typically put mushrooms, uncooked onions, and spicy sauces in a separate container so each family can add what they like.

3. *Plan ahead.* Plan your meals at least three months at a time and print out calendars so everyone knows what's being delivered for dinner each night. List delivery days and times on the meal calendar.

4. *Buy similar containers.* Purchase inexpensive 9-by-13-inch glass baking dishes with plastic snap-on lids at discount stores or garage sales. Use semi-disposable plastic containers and Ziploc bags for sides and sauces. All pans and containers will cycle through the club, so don't expect your exact pans back.

5. *Minister to one another.* Soon after our youngest daughter was born, she was diagnosed with a serious respiratory virus. She was in the hospital for days, and I spent that time with her. My husband went back and forth to the hospital, caring for us and our three older children at home. During that time, my supper-swapping girlfriends delivered meals, cards, and prayers every night for almost two weeks—and I didn't cook a thing for them. It was a blessing to know they were feeding my family when I wasn't able to.

—Trisha Berg, *Today's Christian Woman,* September/October 2006

Q: In the past, our family vacations haven't been too enjoyable. Long car rides, too much fast-food and sleepless nights in motels is not my idea of a good time. What other ways can our family enjoy vacation time together?

A: As my husband and I considered destinations for last summer's vacation, we had this head-slapping realization: *Why not stay home?* We had never taken advantage of the attractions in our own backyard because they were too expensive for everyday play. But we realized that if we funneled the money we had budgeted for travel, hotel accommodations, and eating out into playing tourist in our own town, we'd save major bucks and finally get to enjoy some area attractions.

Here are some things we learned from our first homeward-bound vacation.

• Avoid most daily chores. Use disposable plates and utensils whenever possible for meals. If you're concerned about keeping things neat and tidy during the week, splurge and hire someone to clean your house during that time. Go ahead and collect your mail, but leave the bills untouched. Turn your phones off and let calls go into voice-mail. You're on vacation!

• One of our first stops was our local chamber of commerce, where we picked up glossy pamphlets used to lure tourists to our area. Then we chose a few big outings the entire family would enjoy. If you look around your town, you'll find plenty of free things to do, such as attending outdoor band concerts, art fairs, and music festivals.

• A great girls-only activity (especially for daughters in junior high or high school) is an afternoon at a spa. If that's too pricey, stage a home-based version by lounging all morning in your pajamas drinking fruit smoothies, painting your nails, and doing facials with samples from the mall or ingredients from home.

• How about a trip to a local dollar store? I have yet to meet a child of any age who doesn't thoroughly enjoy spending money at one of these stores. Let them buy souvenirs and disposable cameras so they can snap their own photos throughout the week.

• Order take-out from your favorite restaurants a few times. This is a real budget stretcher since you don't have to pay a tip and there's no temptation to purchase a beverage. If you have older kids, let them choose a restaurant one night. Or send them to the store to buy ingredients for a special meal or a decadent dessert they can fix themselves.

Vacationing at home is one of the smartest things we've done. The cost was minimal and the fun maximum. It reminded us of the importance of playing with our children. Like many parents, we often are guilty of working too much and not enjoying times of rest as God intended—especially Sunday, which can be one of our most exhausting days.

Vacationing at home reminded us that recreation doesn't have to take, well, work.

When you're planning your next family vacation, resist the urge to overbook. Spending time with your kids making special memories doesn't require lots of money or exotic destinations. Keep it simple. Have fun. And remember, "There's no place like home!"

—Theresa Lode, *Today's Christian Woman*, July/August 2003

Q: I've just moved into a new home. What are some easy ways I can get to know my neighbors?

A: Here are some simple ways you can reach out to the people who live near you:

1. *Keep your welcome room clean.* While the rest of your house can be chaotic, try to keep your living room tidy. Having a "safe" spot makes it easier to invite neighbors in for a moment.

2. *Welcome the newbies.* When someone moves onto your street, host a "Welcome to the Neighborhood Dessert." Drop invitations in your neighbors' mailboxes, and serve coffee and cookies. This helps break the ice for the newcomers and gives you the chance to chat with other neighbors.

3. *Bake and break.* When the holidays roll around, host a Christmas cookie exchange. Everyone trades two dozen for an amazing variety to take home, while you all snack on the other half-dozen cookies over a cup of coffee or cocoa.

4. *Eat and run.* Plan a progressive-dinner block party. Everyone brings his/her own plate and silverware, and each participating household hosts the appetizers, salad, main entree, or dessert. This divides the work so no one has too much to do.

5. *Trade your trash.* Organize a Neighborhood Exchange by asking people on your block to donate clothes, toys, or sports equipment their kids have outgrown. Display these items on tables in your backyard and invite your neighbors to rummage through and find some free, slightly used treasures. Donate the leftovers to a local charity.

—Kim Kasch, *Today's Christian Woman*, September/October 2004

Additional Resources:

Books:

The Messies' Manual: A Complete Guide to Bringing Order & Beauty to Your Home,
Sandra Felton (Revell, 2005)

Messie No More: Understanding and Overcoming the Roadblocks to Being Organized,
Sandra Felton (Revell, 2002)

Is There Life After Housework?: A Revolutionary Approach to Cutting Your Cleaning Time 75%,
Don Aslett (Adam's Media Corp., 2005)

Simplify Your Life: Get Organized and Stay That Way,
Marcia Ramsland (Thomas Nelson, 2007)

Busy People's Super Simple 30-Minute Menus,
Dawn Hall (Thomas Nelson, 2007)

Inspirational Home: Simple Ideas for Uplifting Décor and Craft,
Jeanne Winters (Creative Faith Place, 2005)

Websites:

www.flylady.net
Housecleaning and organizing tips with homespun humor

www.housecleaning-tips.com
Housecleaning tips and action plans

www.organizedhome.com
Home maintenance tips and schedules

www.jeannewinters.com
Unique Christian ideas for your home

Questions About

Being Single

Q: Why am I still single, when God knows I long to love and be loved by a good man?

A: Without the earthly companionship you long for, you face a decision. Do you believe, as Eve did when she was tempted in the Garden of Eden (Gen. 3:2–6), that God is cruelly withholding the very thing for which your heart hungers? Or do you believe what God has told you—that He's doing what's best for you even if it hurts and you simply don't understand (Rom. 8:28)?

Perhaps faith in the face of disappointment pleases God because it keeps the ones He loves so close to Him. In Mark 9:17–27, a distraught father brings his suffering son to Jesus to be healed. Jesus asks the man if he believes his boy can be healed, and the man replies, "I do believe; help me overcome my unbelief!" In our darkest times, when we come to the end of ourselves and have tasted loneliness past what we think we're able to bear, we too can cry out to Jesus for help. In resisting the temptation to doubt His goodness toward us, we're brought closer to Him.

God wants a man to love you for the woman He made you to be. He knows that when you give who you really are to the right man, the groundwork will be secure for a powerful union. In the meantime, God will continue to build your faith, increase your reliance on Him, and gently reveal to you who you are—a woman with a great capacity for love and a greater capacity to bring Him glory.

—Colleen Alden. *Today's Christian Woman*, January/February 2005

Q: How can I make the most of being single?

A: In the age of Dr. Phil, we assume that to break out of a marriage rut, a couple needs to spend more time together, invest more in the relationship, or just mix things up a bit. In many ways, the same principles of nurturing a marriage relationship apply to nurturing yourself as a single. Whether you're single for a short time or for a lifetime, try these steps for making the most of your life.

First, ask yourself, "What am I putting on hold?" For whatever reasons you've stalled on these activities, make it a goal to follow through on your list. By doing this, you are investing in you! You are nurturing your individuality and the very gifts and interests that make you uniquely who you are.

Second, listen to what you're saying about your singleness. If your conversations with other single friends center on the negative aspects of being alone, singleness will look like a curse instead of a gift.

Third, keep a list of the positive aspects of being single, and then routinely celebrate those. I keep a Thanksgiving Journal, which I turn to when I need to right my attitude. By reviewing past entries, I'm reminded of all the good things that have happened. Adding new entries helps me notice the good things I'm experiencing right now. Learning to find joy in the ordinary moments of life will serve us well in life, faith, and possibly someday in marriage.

—Camerin Courtney, *SinglesNewsletter* 2005

Happy and Single

Here are some suggestions for making the most of your singleness.

• *Ask around.* Talk to your married friends and find out what they miss most about being single. Girls' nights out? Taking a photography class? Take advantage of these opportunities now so you'll have no regrets later.

• *Make a list.* What do you want to accomplish in life—write a book? Travel to Italy? Participate in a short-term mission trip? Write all these ideas on a master list, then pick one thing and go for it. Don't let waiting for a husband put your life on hold.

• *Pray.* Ecclesiastes chapter 3 tells us there are specific purposes for certain seasons of life. Ask God what unique things He wants you to do in this single season. Obedience to these things will draw you closer to Him and offer you an exciting ride.

• *Invest in others.* Since you're not focusing a majority of your relational energy into a husband right now, you've got a lot to give. There are Sunday school classes, refugee families, and weary neighbors who could be eternally blessed by your involvement in their lives. The joy you'll receive in return will help chase away those lonely days.

• *Get going.* There's a lot to see and do in this big world, and now's your chance to take it all in. A road trip with friends is always a bonding experience. Enrich your life by broadening its boundaries. You never know whom you may meet along the way.

—Camerin Courtney. *Today's Christian Woman*, September/October 1998

INSIGHT

Q: When I was dating as a non-Christian, having sex was normal. Now I'm a committed Christian, and it has been quite a struggle to remain pure. What are some suggestions to help with abstinence?

A: Here are some guidelines:

• *Check him out.* Make sure you and your dating partner have the same commitment to abstinence. Set physical boundaries with your partner, such as not being alone for long periods at a time.

• *Share the struggle.* Communicate with your partner about your struggle, but don't go into detail. Let each other know if you're feeling weak and consider not getting together at that time.

• *Arm yourself with truth.* Read the Bible, Christian books, and Christian articles about sex before marriage and why it isn't appropriate. When you've finished reading everything, read it all again.

• *Be accountable.* Find a trusted friend who shares your beliefs about abstinence and who can pray and talk to you about it and hold you accountable.

• *List the consequences.* Write down how having sex outside of marriage can negatively affect your life. When you're tempted, think of these consequences.

• *Take a break from your dating partner.* Take that time to seek God's guidance and help. Work on yourself and your relationship with God.

—Kel, *SinglesNewsletter* 2005

Q: Is it possible to experience a second virginity, even if I've already had sex?

A: You can lose your physical virginity just once. If you did it, you did it. But spiritually, it is quite possible to start over again.

Spiritual rebirth doesn't destroy the past; it transforms it. The God who made the universe out of nothing can take your past and make something beautiful of it. You can't manage that transformation on your own; you need God's power and forgiveness. You find that by asking for it.

Spiritual transformation begins as simply and as mysteriously as that. Perhaps you are no longer a virgin in the physical sense. But because you have been purified by God, you are a virgin in His eyes. That may not clear up your reputation or your memory, but it does clear up your future with God. You are as good as new.

Once you've experienced God's forgiveness, you'll still have to deal with the leftovers of your past, such as guilt. Like other natural consequences— pregnancy, disease, or painful memories—feelings don't necessarily disappear when God transforms your life. But their sting is taken away. So, even though you may still feel guilty about past sexual relationships, it's vital to know that, as far as God is concerned, you're not guilty. God promises to forgive us and cleanse us when we confess our sins to Him (see 1 John 1:9).

Jesus didn't die on the cross to take away your feelings. He died to take away your sins. Cleansed of sin, you can work on transforming your feelings into becoming a useful tool for God's service.

—Tim Stafford, *Campus Life*, January/February, 2001

Q: In my past, I was promiscuous. I partied and got married and divorced twice. Now that I'm a Christian, I want to honor God in my dating relationships, but every Christian man I've met is scared off by my past. How can I rebuild my reputation?

A: It's not easy to make a clean break with the past. Even though you know God forgives and forgets, sometimes it feels like others won't give you a chance.

You might consider taking yourself "off the market" for a while. Take time to strengthen your relationship with God. Get grounded in the Word.

Develop healthy friendships with more mature believers—especially women—who can offer accountability and support.

Do everything you can to build a solid foundation for your growing faith by creating new, healthy patterns to replace the old ones.

When you begin dating again, resist the urge to come clean about everything you've ever done—at least right away. (Remember it's a date, not a therapy session). It's enough to say simply, "I haven't always been a Christian. I've made mistakes in my past." Maybe even, "I've been married before." But then move on to what God is doing in your life now. Let your date get to know you as a person and see the wonderful woman you are becoming in Christ before sharing your past.

—Christin Ditchfield, *Today's Christian Woman*, July/August 2006

Q: I'm thirty-seven years old and recently started seeing a nice Christian guy. He has been divorced for two years (his wife had an affair and left him), and he's honest about missing the physical aspect of that relationship. I know God doesn't approve of premarital sex, but I think this man could be Mr. Right and, at my age, I'm struggling with the whole idea of "true love waits." Any advice?

A: Sexual intercourse draws us into the profound mystery of "one flesh." It's meant to bond a man and a woman in a deep and wonderful way. But sex outside the lifelong covenant of permanence and fidelity sets up expectations and creates needs that almost always dismantle the relationship.

The problem with using sex as a means to increase intimacy before marriage is that it soon becomes a substitute for emotional intimacy. Couples who put their sexuality on fast-forward, short-circuit the normal progression of linking hearts and souls.

Research shows the emotional bonding required for lasting love is most likely to move slowly and systematically through stages. For a relationship to achieve its full potential, it must be nourished by emotional vulnerability and countless private memories. Having sex too soon keeps those things from developing. It creates an illusion of intimacy that fades with the fires of passion.

So hold onto your resolve to hold out for sex until you're married. Your Mr. Right knows from experience the deep value of fidelity in a relationship. And he certainly knows about infidelity's destructive power to dismantle one.

—Leslie Parrott, *Today's Christian Woman*, May/June 2006

Q: My ten-year-old son doesn't want me to date. How can I help him adjust to this new relationship?

A: *Pray together.* Specifically, pray for the man God may bring into Mommy's life. This gives your child a sense of being involved so that when you begin to build friendships with men, your child isn't quite so threatened by it.

Second, *provide reassurance.* Your son is probably used to having you all to himself and doesn't want to share. Explain that you need friends just like he does, but that doesn't mean you love him any less. Above all, listen to your child. His thoughts and feelings are very real. To keep your son from feeling left out, plan something special for him to do when you're on a date, such as visiting a friend or seeing a ball game.

Finally, *don't rush it.* Your son will need some time to adjust. Meet your date on more neutral territory, like at a movie theater or restaurant. Wait until the relationship becomes more serious to introduce your friend to your son. When the time is right, plan activities that you know your son will enjoy. Give your son the chance to interact with your boyfriend in a fun, comfortable environment. The more positive interactions your son has with your boyfriend, the more he may be willing to accept your new relationship.

—Reader responses, *Christian Parenting Today,* November/December 2000

Q: How can I support my friend who is going through a divorce?

A: Divorce disrupts the emotional and spiritual life of a family as well as the financial side. Listen to what your friend may not be saying. Maybe your friend has a very simple, practical need you can meet. If you can offer minor handyman repairs or occasional childcare, let your friend know you're willing to do this.

People who divorce often feel like failures; they are hurting, angry, and lonely. Whether or not we agree with their decisions to end their marriages, they need a big dose of unconditional love and hope rather than condemnation. Friends can encourage divorced people to pay attention to what God is telling them through this experience.

Gently nourish your friend's creative side. When so many dreams have died, our God-given spark of creativity often seems buried, too. Time pressures can make creative work seem like a luxury we can ill afford. Yet when we most need a reason to feel alive again and to have a new purpose for our lives, discovering new artistic or creative abilities can be energizing. God may be calling us to develop gifts we've neglected or ignored.

Perhaps you can help by offering to baby-sit once in a while so your friend can explore new hobbies, interests, or talents. Or you might invite your friend to ride with you to a class or meeting, saving money for gas.

Good friends give hope, strength, and love at a time when help is desperately needed. Friends encourage divorced people to find the freedom of forgiveness and the ability to dream again.

—Judy Corey, *Today's Christian Woman*, November/December 1997

Q: I'm a single mom and have to work to keep food on the table. I'm exhausted by the time I pick up my kids at daycare, and I don't feel I'm giving my two girls much quality time. Their dad is pretty much out of the picture. Any suggestions on how to be a better mom?

A: Lose the guilt. That's easier said than done, I know. But try taking a look at your inadequacy from God's perspective. He says to the apostle Paul in 2 Corinthians 12:9, "My grace is all you need. My power works best in weakness" (NLT).

A verse I hold tightly when I'm feeling like a failure as a mother is Isaiah 54:13: "All your children shall be taught by the LORD, and great shall be the peace of your children" (NKJV). Isn't it comforting to remember it isn't all up to us? First and foremost, our babies are God's children, and He loves them even more than we do.

With this understanding of God's desire and His ability to take what you have to give as a mom and make it sufficient, perhaps you'll eventually be able to say with the apostle Paul: "I am glad to boast about my weaknesses, so that the power of Christ can work through me. That's why I take pleasure in my weaknesses, and in the insults, hardships, persecutions, and troubles that I suffer for" (2 Cor. 12:9–10 NLT).

—Lisa Whelchel, *Today's Christian Woman*, March/April 2004

Q: I was widowed a few years ago. Though I have no desire to remarry, I would like at least to have some companionship with the opposite sex. But these thoughts make me feel disloyal to my late husband. What should I do?

A: When a successful relationship is broken, the surviving partner feels disoriented, much like an amputee.

It's up to the surrounding community to offer the bereaved a role that is useful, honorable, and fulfilling. You're not getting this; few single people in our culture do, since pairing up is relentlessly presented as the only choice. Singles are continually pushed together and prompted to find a mate, as if anything short of couple-life is deficient.

Christians desperately need to recover a way of seeing the single life as valid on its own terms and not simply as a holding tank. Though never-marrieds are made to feel like failures, that would hardly be history's judgment of our great example, the apostle Paul. He found his singleness so fulfilling that he said, "I wish that all men were even as I myself" (1 Cor. 7:7 NKJV).

Today there is so much cultural impatience with singleness that we can stand to put more weight on the other side of the scale. God's grace is more than sufficient to see us through our bouts of loneliness. However, you should feel no guilt for desiring companionship. Ask God to fill the emptiness you're feeling. His answer may not be what you expect, but it's always the best.

—Frederica Mathewes-Green, *Today's Christian Woman*, January/February 2005

Additional Resources

Books:

Alone with God: Biblical Inspiration for the Unmarried,
Michael Warden (Barbour, 2002).

Finding Your Million Dollar Mate, Randy Pope (Northfield, 2004).

Define the Relationship: A Candid Look at Breaking Up, Making Up, and Dating Well,
Jeramy and Jerusha Clark (WaterBrook Press, 2004).

Boundaries in Dating: Making Dating Work, Dr. Henry Cloud & Dr. John Townsend
(Zondervan, 2000).

Living Whole Without a Better Half, Wendy Widder (Kregel, 2000).

When God Writes Your Love Story: The Ultimate Approach to Guy/Girl Relationships,
Eric & Leslie Ludy (Multnomah, 2004).

Sassy, Single, and Satisfied: Secrets to Loving the Life You're Living,
Michelle McKinney Hammond (Harvest House, 2003).

Table for One: The Savvy Girl's Guide to Singleness, Camerin Courtney (Baker, 2002).

Revelations of a Single Woman: Loving the Life I Didn't Expect, Connally Gilliam (SaltRiver, 2006).

Websites:

www.TodaysChristianWoman.com.
Great resources for Christian single women by *Today's Christian Woman* magazine

www.ChristianSinglesToday.com
A website for singles by Christianity Today International

www.ChristianWomenOnline.net General site for Christian women

www.singleness.org
Comprehensive website offers inspiration, encouragement, and support for
Christian singles who desire to live purposeful lives for Jesus Christ

Questions About

Marriage

Q: I'm newly married and have a lot of interests that don't include my husband (playing sports, volunteering at church, taking dance lessons). But I always have to negotiate to get to do them. I feel as if he wants me to give up all the things I enjoy. How can I do the things I love without feeling guilty or starting a major war?

A: One of the most common mistakes many of us make is to incorrectly interpret what our partner doesn't say and then function as if that assumption is truth. Has your husband clearly told you he wants you to give up all the things you enjoy, or is that your interpretation? Is it possible you've made some incorrect assumptions?

This may sound like a small first step, but overgeneralization and all-or-nothing thinking result in exaggeration and inflation of a problem, which leads to discouragement and frustration. I suggest you communicate to your spouse in clear and unambiguous ways your specific concerns and let him know explicitly what you'd like to see change. What are some things you enjoy doing together? What are some things you like to do by yourself? Start with one or two that would be most meaningful.

Marriage does involve sacrifice. The biggest adjustment for many couples is going from "I" thinking to "we" thinking. That doesn't mean giving up your uniqueness. While it's important to maintain some individual interests, it's also vital that you and your husband discover things you enjoy doing together. It's easy for some couples to function as "married singles" and expect their lives to be basically the same as they were before they were married.

—Gary and Carrie Oliver, *Marriage Partnership*, Summer 2006

Q: My husband and I have a healthy sex life, but I feel like we're missing out on intimacy in other ways. Is sex the only way we really become one?

A: God designed marriage to be the most intimate of human relationships, in which we share life intellectually, socially, emotionally, spiritually, and physically. It's possible you don't feel like you're experiencing complete intimacy with your husband because you're overlooking other ways we can be known. Here are some:

• *Intellectual intimacy.* The important thing is discussing your thoughts. They may be impression or opinions about food, finances, health, work, or politics.

• *Social intimacy.* When we do things together, we not only develop a sense of teamwork, but we also enhance our sense of intimacy.

• *Emotional intimacy.* Feelings are spontaneous, emotional responses to what we encounter through the five senses. When we share emotions, we build emotional intimacy.

• *Spiritual intimacy.* Often the least excavated of all forms of marital intimacy, it doesn't require agreement of belief on every detail. Instead, we seek to tell each other what's going on in our inner self.

• *Physical intimacy.* Because men and women are different, we come at sexual intimacy in different ways. The husband's emphasis is often on the physical aspects—the seeing, touching, and climax. The wife comes to sexual intimacy with more interest in the relationship. To feel loved, appreciated, and treated tenderly brings her great joy. Sexual intimacy requires understanding and responding to these differences.

—Gary D. Chapman, *Marriage Partnership*, Fall 2005

Q: We've been married five years and I desperately want to have children, but my husband says "no." I feel I've been duped, since he said "maybe" to children before we were married. Whenever I bring up the topic, he shuts down. We're at an impasse. What can I do?

A: The decision about having children can be difficult for married couples. When we hit a brick wall in dealing with the core of our heart's desires, it's important to step back to stop, look, and listen.

From your question it sounds as though the only options are for one of you to give in and perhaps be bitter, or to continue in this stalemate. Neither will help you reach a solution and strengthen your marriage.

The bigger issue here involves discerning God's desire for your marriage. It isn't just about whether or not to have children; it's about what it takes to serve, cherish, and encourage each other in the context of dealing with an emotionally charged issue. As we've seen in our own marriage and in countless other marriages, God can make a huge difference in situations like these if we're willing to make understanding our spouse and listening for God's voice more important than merely winning our point.

Given the significance and potential volatility of this issue, we encourage you to see a trained marriage counselor. You need someone who can be objective in helping you both walk through your concerns. Deepening your understanding of each other's desires, fears, and wants will help you reach a decision you both can embrace.

—Carrie and Gary J. Oliver, *Marriage Partnership*, Summer 2006

Q: I thought having a baby would draw my husband and me together and we'd be happy. But since the baby came, our marriage has fallen apart. I'm up to my ears in diapers and vomit, and he's grumbling because I don't bake cherry pies anymore. What can we do?

A: In my experience, the issues most likely to provoke conflict between a husband and wife—in any stage of parenting—are: division of work load, lack of couple time, a frustrating sexual relationship, money management, the need for time alone, in-laws, and differing child rearing strategies. The following are some ways a couple can grow through these challenges:

1. Make marriage a priority. Most of us recognize that a strong, loving marriage is one of the greatest gifts we can give our children. So why not begin by deciding to put your marriage on the front burner?

2. Share your decision with your spouse. Maybe he'll join you, welcoming the idea of making marriage a priority. He's likely as frustrated as you with the present situation.

3. Individually make a list of the things you enjoyed most before the children came. Share your lists with each other and relive some of the moments you enjoyed in that stage of marriage.

4. List five things that would improve your marriage right now. Evaluate them by placing the word *realistic*, *unrealistic*, or *maybe* beside each. Share your lists. See if you can agree on at least one thing from each that you'll attempt to do this week.

—Gary D. Chapman, *Marriage Partnership*, Winter 2005

Q: Since we purchased a business two years ago, it has consumed more and more of my husband's time. Six days a week he is gone by 7:00 a.m. and doesn't return home until midnight or later. Our kids are growing up without him, and I am desperately lonely. Should I urge him to sell the business?

A: Before you suggest selling the business, consider some alternatives. For starters, realize that your husband is working hard to support his family and to make the business succeed. Not all men take those responsibilities so seriously. So as you discuss a solution, I hope you'll focus on the business—not your husband—as the problem.

To help reduce the number of hours he is away from home, perhaps you and your children could help out with the business. That would reduce your husband's work stress and also would give you more time together.

At the same time, your husband should seek advice from a fellow professional. Something is wrong if he is working seventeen hours a day. Perhaps another businessman could offer insights that would increase efficiency and reduce your husband's workload.

Meanwhile, even though you're lonely, try to support your husband. A few years ago, a U.S. Air Force study determined why some military kids go bad while others do so well. The essential factor turned out to be how supportive the military spouse, usually a wife, was.

Eventually your family may have to sell the business. But first, see if you and your husband can make it work by making some changes and seeking outside advice.

—Jay Kesler, *Marriage Partnership*, Winter 1997

Q: I thought coming into a new marriage after my last one ended in divorce would be like starting with a clean slate. Instead, I'm finding a lot of the same issues resurfacing from my former marriage. How do I move forward and change these patterns?

A: The fairy-tale view of a second marriage assumes that all the mistakes and pain from the first marriage are ancient history. Reality hits as couples realize the new marriage, just like the last one, has big challenges. Some are brand-new, such as getting a feel for each other as new husband and wife while also trying to parent one or two sets of kids. Some challenges are reruns, such as staying angry at a former spouse and not realizing what that anger is doing to the new marriage. Here are some to watch out for:

1. Memory triggers. If something your first spouse did made you feel betrayed, then recognize that as a rotten plank and make your new spouse aware of it, lest he unknowingly trips your trigger with similar behavior.

2. Forgive. Many a second marriage has been doomed by lingering pain, especially if the marriage has come too soon after a divorce or a spouse's death for enough healing time. Rely on God, not on your new marriage, to purge your life of past bitterness. That includes forgiving anyone who helped end the previous marriage.

3. Genuine repentance before God is needed for your new marriage to be healthy. Ask God to forgive you for the part you played in the breakdown of the former marriage. Finally, commit to God to make your new marriage last a lifetime.

—Jim Killam, *Marriage Partnership*, Spring 2004

MARRIAGE

Q: I'm in a second marriage, and the holidays are just the worst because that's when my husband's teens visit (his ex-wife has custody). There's a lot of tension between his children and our children, and they compete for attention. It's placing stress on our relationship. What can I do?

A: Mixing children from two different marriages often causes quite a bit of tension. Hard work and good communication are necessary for the various relationships to mesh well.

As the adults, you and your husband need to set the tone for all the children and their respective relationships. So think about how you'd like the children to relate to each other. What are your goals for your time together? What characteristics would you like to nurture in the children? How can you two work together to help both sets of children grow in love and respect for each other?

As you discuss these issues, consider how you help or hinder your children from relating effectively. Do you have any resentment toward the older children? Do you wish they wouldn't come to your home? Does your husband feel guilty about not seeing more of them, so he either distances himself or gives them excessive attention? Hidden attitudes such as these can leak out and infect your home's atmosphere. As you and your husband establish goals and examine your attitudes, pray together for yourselves and each child.

Help your younger children prepare for the visit of your husband's teens well in advance. Perhaps they could send notes or cards to them throughout the year. Teach them about hospitality—what God says about it, and how they might demonstrate it at Christmas.

—Diane Mandt Langberg, *Today's Christian Woman*, November/December 1997

MARRIAGE

Q: Although I was a Christian before I married thirteen years ago, I was sexually active with my spouse before marriage. Now that our kids are preteens, we want to teach them to remain sexually pure. My husband doesn't want me to tell them about our mistakes, but I'm not sure that's the right approach. How should I handle this situation?

A: Unfortunately, it's not uncommon for married couples in your circumstance never to have confessed their premarital sexual activity as sin, which means they also haven't sought and received God's forgiveness. If you haven't done this, search God's Word about sin and forgiveness, then go to Him about the matter.

Every sin is against God—but sexual sin also goes against someone else. While Scripture teaches us to confess our sins to God, it also teaches that we need to confess and seek forgiveness on a human level. You'll need to accept your responsibility for your sin without blaming or resenting your husband, then seek his forgiveness. This may be difficult, especially if he doesn't respond in kind. But focus on doing what's right before God for the sake of your relationship to God, your husband, and your children.

Once you've done the above, you're ready to teach your children what God says about sex—without hesitation or guilt. I don't think your children need to know about your sexual history. What they do need to know are the physical aspects of sex, that God created it, that it's good, and that He has specific instructions on how to manage that area of their lives. They also need to know this is an area they're free to discuss with you.

—Diane Mandt Langberg, *Today's Christian Woman,* January/February 1997

MARRIAGE

Q: I have so many negative emotions toward my spouse. Is there anything I can do to find healing and feel better about my husband?

A: There is hope for overcoming your negative emotions and getting to a better place in your marriage. Here are some ways to respond:

1. Name your negative feelings. Be specific. You may even want to write those impressions down.

2. Ask yourself, "What caused my feelings?" Often there's both an external and an internal source.

3. Make a covenant with God that, with His help, you won't allow your negative emotions to lead you to destructive behavior. Pray for God's wisdom. It may lead you to take some of the following actions.

4. If there are certain circumstances (external sources) that typically create negative outcomes, like habitual lateness, check in with your husband during the day and ask, "How do things look for tonight?" Whatever his response, you are prepared with the information you need to change your own attitude and expectations.

5. Call a truce. If a battle erupts, hold your thoughts before one of you destroys the other, and ask to talk about it later or the next day after you're both rested.

6. Negotiate. Negotiation allows us to share the negative emotions we feel, give our spouse an opportunity to explain his or her behavior, and resolve the issue. It requires listening with the intent to understand and reconcile.

—Gary D. Chapman, *Marriage Partnership*, Winter 2004

MARRIAGE

Q: When I married my husband, I thought he was perfect; everything he did was adorable. Now, some of his behaviors drive me crazy. Will I ever get him to change?

A: We can't demand change; we request change. Knowing this, try these three steps and see if your husband is more receptive to making some changes.

Step 1: *Choose your setting.* By setting I mean time, place, and your mate's feelings. The ideal time is after a meal, since few people respond well when hungry. The place should be private, never public. And always consider your mate's feelings. Is he or she emotionally ready to receive a suggestion tonight?

Step 2: *Don't overdose.* If you tell your spouse five things that irritate you all on the same night, you will kill his motivation to change. Try one request every two weeks. That's twenty-six a year. The husband can make his request one week, and the wife can make hers the next.

Step 3: *Give compliments along with your request.* When your husband knows you like him and you think he's a good man, he'll be more motivated to do better.

Your spouse will never do everything the way you desire, even if you follow the three-steps above. If your spouse hasn't turned off the lights in fifteen years, he may never. Maybe you need to understand that he's the light-turner-on-er, and you're the light-turner-off-er.

—Gary D. Chapman, *Marriage Partnership*, Fall 2004

Q: How do I know if my husband is a sex addict? We've been married a year and all he wants to do is have sex. Is this normal, or does he have a problem?

A: Your husband is probably just a normal male. Studies have found that men think about sex every few minutes. Be happy he's directing that desire toward you, and work together to make your sexual play the most exciting and fulfilling possible.

We know couples who get into arguments over libido issues, in which one spouse, to get the upper hand, will throw out, "You're a sex addict," or "You're a pervert. All you think about is sex." We can't begin to tell you how damaging that is to marriage—and to your spouse's self-esteem. It's cruel. God designed men to have stronger sex drives.

Usually sexual addiction is marked by self-focused involvement with pornography, self-stimulation, or promiscuity. If you have reasons to think these practices exist, express your concern—at a time when foreplay isn't in process!—and ask him directly about his sexual practices.

That said, it's important for you to let your husband know how you're feeling about sex. It would be better for you to negotiate frequency of intercourse than for you to become bitter about his advances.

—Melissa and Louis McBurney, *Marriage Partnership*, Winter 2006

Q: When we make love, we both wonder why we don't do this more often, but our frequency averages about once a month. We don't seem to have the time or energy. How can we overcome this ongoing problem?

A: While men are usually ready for sex more frequently, most women have a more receptive or responsive desire. They won't think of sex as often as a man, but if the thought or activity is initiated, they can enter in with enjoyment. If these differences in desire, along with the dampening effects of inertia and fatigue, are not understood, husbands and wives can feel frustrated, pressured, hurt, and bitter.

In a study of more than two thousand Christian women, the number-one sexual problem was not lack of desire, but fatigue. Most wives don't respond positively to the suggestion of lovemaking at 10:30 at night after a tiring day! Husbands, also weary from many demands, don't think about sex until bedtime.

Some possible ways to improve your love life:

1. List your optimal times for lovemaking and plan definite times for connection. Create spontaneity and variety within these time parameters.

2. List your most common sexual saboteurs. How will you counter them? Need more energy? A strategic nap? A lock on the bedroom door? An enforced bedtime for the children? (Or for you?)

3. If you are the partner with a lower desire for sex, become more intentional about having it. Many women have found help by writing "TS" ("Think Sex") on their calendar.

—Douglas Rosenau and Debra Taylor, *Marriage Partnership*, Winter 2005

MARRIAGE

Q: Every time my husband and I argue, he tries to initiate sex—as though making love will make our anger magically disappear. Why would he think that? And how can I get him to deal with the real issue at hand instead of jumping into bed for "make-up" sex?

A: Men are so compartmentalized about sexual pleasure that many really do believe a tumble in the hay is just the ticket for conflict resolution. It works for them. A good ejaculation and their epinephrine and endorphins mellow them out. The anger and unhappiness of a few minutes ago are erased. Then they're absolutely dumbfounded that their mate is still upset.

Hopefully, with better communication, your husband can begin to understand you. Sometimes it helps to read together a good book about men and women such as *Men Are from Mars, Women Are from Venus* (HarperCollins, 1993), or talk to another couple about this pattern.

The timing is crucial when talking to your spouse. Don't try talking in the heat of a disagreement. Find a time when you're feeling pleasant and relatively stress free. You might begin by telling him there's something you can't figure out and need his help. Then share how important it is for your sexual arousal to have good amorous feelings and that stress or anger or even distractions by the kids really make it difficult for you to switch gears. If there's something he can't do when he's anxious or uptight—if his golf game suffers, for instance—use that to make your point. From there go on to discuss your sexual responsiveness.

—Melissa and Louis McBurney, *Marriage Partnership*, Winter 2006

Additional Resources
Books:

The Marriage You've Always Wanted,
Gary D. Chapman (Moody, 2005)

I Promise: How Five Commitments Determine the Destiny of Your Marriage,
Dr. Gary Smalley (Thomas Nelson, 2007)

Marriage: From Surviving to Thriving,
Charles R. Swindoll (Thomas Nelson, 2006).

Courtship After Marriage: Romance Can Last a Lifetime,
Zig Ziglar (Thomas Nelson, 2004)

Rekindling the Romance: Loving the Love of Your Life,
Dennis and Barbara Rainey (Thomas Nelson, 2004)

Daily Reflections for Stepparents: Living and Loving in a New Family,
Margaret Broersma (Kregel, 2003)

Websites:

www.liferelationships.com
Carrie Oliver is a marriage and family counselor. Gary J. Oliver, Ph.D., co-author of
A Woman's Forbidden Emotion (Regal, 2005), is executive director
of The Center for Relationship Enrichment at John Brown University

www.sexualwholeness.com
Douglas Rosenau and Debra Taylor are sex therapists with Sexual Wholeness, Inc.

www.realrelationships.com
Drs. Les and Leslie Parrott are founders of The Center for Relationship Development
at Seattle Pacific University

Questions About

Parenting
& Children

Q: Our kids drive us nuts at church, so we have stopped going. Some people say that we should go anyway, but we think God understands if we wait to go back until our children are older. Doesn't He?

A: If you're asking if God understands what it's like to parent unruly children who won't sit still and just listen, absolutely He does. He has been parenting billions of us since Creation.

But I think He wants our kids to be a part of the fellowship of believers that makes up church. When the disciples tried to keep the children away from Jesus, I'm sure they were just trying to keep things quiet and focused. Since Jesus invited the children to be with Him, it shows He didn't mind a little wiggle and squirm in His presence.

I understand your concern. Until my kids got used to the nursery and then their own children's worship, I spent much more time digging through my cavernous purse for gummy fruit snacks, crayons, and toys than I did in any kind of meaningful worship.

Then an older mom filled me in on something. She told me to stop focusing on church being an opportunity to get "fed" and to concentrate on bringing my children to God's house as a way of training them up in the Lord. While I wasn't learning much during church, I was glorifying God by bringing my squirmy kids there. And she was right.

—Caryn Rivadeneira, "Ask a Resourceful Mom," February 2006, www.todayschristianwoman.com

Q: Our four-year-old daughter falls asleep in her own bed, but she always climbs into bed with us during the night. Is this okay?

A: The only way to sort through all of the widely varying theories on co-sleeping is to determine what works best for your family. Start by asking yourself if your daughter's presence in your bed is disrupting the sleep habits of you and your husband. If sleeping with your four-year-old is like sleeping with most children, who tend to be restless, wiggly, and noisy, then it likely interferes with your sleep.

You also need to talk with your husband about this issue. Men (and women, too) can resent the presence of a child in the bed because of the impact the child has on both sleep and sex.

The ability to soothe oneself to sleep is an important developmental growth marker for kids. So ask some questions about your daughter's general sleep patterns. If your child has never had a sustained time period (six months or more) of independent sleeping (getting herself to sleep, falling back to sleep without parental intervention), then by age three, you've already got a problem on your hands.

If you feel it's time to move your daughter out of your bed, you'll need to deal with your feelings about the change. Rather than thinking of yourself as a mean mom for sending your child back to her own bed, tell yourself the truth—your child needs to learn to comfort herself at night and stay in her bed while doing so.

—Karen L. Maudlin, *Christian Parenting Today*, Summer 2004

PARENTING & CHILDREN

Q: Sibling rivalry is driving me crazy. My kids are constantly squabbling with each other. How can my husband and I eliminate this behavior?

A: Sibling rivalry is as old as the Old Testament account of Cain and Abel (Genesis 4), and families experience its frustrations every day. Here are some tools to keep your kids from driving you and each other crazy, as well as to help them learn to become friends.

The Early Years (Ages 1–10). Think of yourself as a coach who's training your kids in the fundamentals of getting along. Try these practical tips to make this stage easier:

1. *Prepare for a new baby.* Older siblings often misbehave when Mom is caring for a new baby. Offset jealousy by planning dates with your older kids without the baby. Get a babysitter and take a trip to the movies or an ice cream shop.

2. *Promote sharing.* An argument over who gets to sit next to the window on a three-minute car ride can start a war. Solve this dilemma by assigning one child the odd-numbered days; the other, the even-numbered days. On a child's assigned day, he gets first choice at everything all day long. (If you have more than two children, assign one child every third or fourth day.)

3. *Teach respect.* Teach your kids to argue fairly instead of resorting to personal attacks. A child who is allowed to get away with verbal abuse will develop into a teen who talks back to parents and teachers as well as a spouse who verbally abuses his wife and kids.

The Middle Years (ages 11–16). When you reach this stage, you'll need to approach it more as a referee than coach:

1. *Decide when to get involved.* As you watch your children interact, cheer their good moves, ache when they falter, and encourage them to solve some of their own conflicts.

2. *Hold family forums.* If your kids are experiencing repeated discord, gather your family together and insist that each person listen as other family members express views about the problem. Then discuss creative solutions: "Can you think of three creative ways to handle this problem? If you were the parent, how would you handle this dispute?"

3. *Encourage togetherness.* Often siblings who clash do so because they're competing for your attention. So give these "clashers" a chance to spend time together without you around. This is especially helpful when you're trying to blend siblings from two different families.

—Susan Alexander Yates, *Today's Christian Woman,* May/June 2000

Q: My daughter and I continually have communication breakdowns that end with her running from the room, crying, "You just don't understand; it's no use talking to you about it." What can I do to improve our communication?

A: All moms long for good communication with their kids, but the reality is that good communication won't happen unless you cultivate an atmosphere of acceptance in your home. The following actions will help you create an environment that encourages parent-child communication.

1. *Make time for them.* True communication grows out of the relational groundwork you create when your children are young. Set aside daily time with each child. Read him or her a story or go for a walk. As they grow older, you can't program time when a teen will want to talk. You have to hang around just in case the urge strikes. When it does, it will probably be inconvenient for you, but setting aside your own agenda to listen to your child is well worth the inconvenience.

2. *Teach respect.* At some point, most kids try to talk back to their parents and siblings. Don't permit it. Teach your children how to disagree with you and with each other without resorting to verbal abuse.

3. *Walk in their world.* The carpool can be a great research tool. The kids forget you're there. So just keep quiet and listen and learn.

4. *Open your home to their friends.* Put out lots of food—and they will come. You may have to cancel your social life during the teen years, but it's more important that you have your teen's friends at your house, where you can control what goes on.

—Susan Alexander Yates, *Today's Christian Woman*, July/August 2001

Q: My kids are in elementary school. They seem a little young to learn about sex. When should we give "the talk"? What should we say?

A: Most of us would rather face a root canal than talk to our kids about sex. It can be awkward, difficult, not to mention embarrassing. Here are some guidelines to help you tackle this all-important parenting task.

1. *Talk more than once.* When you have the first talk with your child, keep it simple. Share facts and use proper terminology. Be sure to encourage questions. Don't give more information than the children need. Reassure them you'll have many conversations about this as they grow older and that you want them to feel free to ask you anything, anytime. No question is dumb.

In follow-up discussions, don't talk only about sex. Sex isn't an isolated issue, so be sure to discuss commitment, communication, choosing a mate, marriage, and having children.

2. *Communicate the positives.* In a world that cheapens sex, we need to elevate it. Make sure you communicate its goodness in the context of marriage to your children. And be sure to take your kids to God's Word to teach its standards about sex.

3. *Be forgiving.* Some parents have deep regrets about their sexual past. Prayerfully consider whether you should share this aspect of your experience. If God gives you the green light, go ahead. Be quick to remind yourselves and your children of God's grace. There is no sin He cannot forgive. He is a God of fresh starts.

—Susan Alexander Yates, *Today's Christian Woman,* May/June 1999

Q: Our teenage daughter wants to date a great Christian guy who happens to be of another race. I'm OK with that, but my husband, also a Christian, is adamantly opposed. I don't want to tolerate my husband's racism, yet I don't want to undermine his leadership role in our family. What should I do?

A: Racism is an ugly thing; in no way does it reflect the mind of Christ toward His creatures. To exhibit prejudice of any kind is to misrepresent the character of God in this world.

But there's another possible reason your husband might be concerned about your teen dating someone of another race: Love relationships and marriage are difficult enough without the added complexity of racial differences. The truth is, however, that sometimes people hide their prejudice behind such statements, so this matter is complicated.

Due to this issue's complexity, I recommend you and your husband seek outside counsel. If your spouse's attitude is sinful, it's a good idea to have a pastor or Christian counselor involved in confronting him. A third party can also help you learn to respond to your husband and to your daughter in a way that doesn't further divide your family.

Tell your daughter that her request to date this young man has posed some difficulties for the two of you. Explain that you're going to seek help in understanding and resolving this dilemma. In the meantime, ask her not to date the young man until you've worked it out. It's crucial you discuss this with her as a team because it prevents your daughter from playing one parent against the other.

—Diane Mandt Langberg, *Today's Christian Woman*, July/August 1998

Q: My son just started high school. He hasn't given much thought to college yet, but I'm starting to feel pressure to plan for his future schooling. Is it too soon to be concerned about college? What can I do to prepare for this milestone?

A: Today college pressure begins as early as the ninth grade. That's the year your child's GPA begins to count. Chances are, your child will start looking at colleges his first semester of junior year or even as soon as the second semester of his sophomore year. While senior year is normally application time, most applications usually have to be submitted by December. Here are a few things that may help you and your child plan for life after high school.

• *Make joint decisions.* Sure, your kids still need some parameters in making decisions, but they need a say in where they want to go to school. So decide together on approximately five colleges to apply to. If your child's not gung-ho about attending college, brainstorm two non-college options about which you both feel comfortable.

• *Make visits.* Make sure you visit the campus with your child, especially if you've never seen the school. If possible, arrange for your child to spend the night in a dorm with a believer.

Too often we research the best academic fit for our child but fail to research the potential for spiritual growth. In the long run, it's spiritual growth that's most crucial. Encourage your son to attend classes the next day. He'll get a more realistic picture of college life mid-week than on weekends.

—Susan Alexander Yates, *Today's Christian Woman,* March/April 1999

Q: My kids are involved in several different activities. While they are all positive, sometimes I wonder if we would do well to just let them play around the house sometimes. How do you know if you're over-scheduling your child?

A: Through free play, a child learns to function within his peer group, make rules, test the limits of acceptable behavior, and role-play future occupations. Dr. Michael Stern, a child psychologist at Tod Children's Hospital in Youngstown, Ohio, suggests parents do an inventory of their child's schedule of extracurricular activities and consider the following:

• How many hours a day is your child in school?

• How many hours a day does your child participate in sports, music, dance, art, or other after-school activities?

• How much homework does he average each night?

• How much sleep is he getting? The recommended ten hours?

Once you have an idea of how much time your child is spending in these areas, prioritize his time. Start with the activities the child must do, such as homework, chores, and time at night to read the Bible or do a family devotion, or sleep. Then prioritize the extra activities your child is involved in according to which ones he enjoys most. Help your child determine what should stay and what should go. Stern advises parents to use their judgment in eliminating activities, and to strive for a least one hour of unstructured time each day.

—Mary Ellen Pellegrini, *Christian Parenting Today*, March/April 2002

Q: Our culture's standard for integrity seems to be: It doesn't matter if you shade the truth as long as no one gets hurt and you don't get caught. What can we do to raise kids with God's standard for integrity?

A: While it's difficult to uphold God's standard in our fallen world, here are five suggestions that may help you raise your kids to be people of integrity:

1. *Model honesty.* It's easy to exaggerate or use white lies for convenience sake, such as asking your child to tell a telephone caller you're not home when you are.

2. *Don't blame others.* When something goes wrong, our natural instinct is to blame others—our boss, our circumstances, our friends. Teach your child that in the final analysis, she is responsible for her own behavior.

3. *Discipline lying.* Talk with your children about honesty. Make sure they understand lying will result in big punishment. If your child is caught in a lie, don't bail him out. Walk with him in his punishment, but let him suffer the consequences of his actions.

4. *Praise integrity.* Tell your kids the most important thing they can do is to tell the truth. Then, when they do, praise them for it.

5. *Follow the right standard.* Television, movies, and videos often wink at lying, cheating, and deception. We must look to God's Word as our standard, not to other people.

—Susan Alexander Yates, *Today's Christian Woman*, July/August 2002

Q: I feel uncomfortable letting my preteen go with her friends to the park where I can't see them, or walk some distance away to get ice cream. But this is what kids do in my area. What are the right boundaries to set for her age?

A: It's important to talk to other parents about your community's safety issues and to listen to your instincts on what is or isn't safe. But here are some general principles to help you determine some guidelines for your daughter:

• Develop a written list of do's and don'ts about where she can go and what she can do. Be sure to review it annually.

• Have kids travel in groups. A lone kid of any age is vulnerable to a predator.

• Stroll around your neighborhood with your child and talk through safety issues. Secluded areas are to be avoided. Populated and lighted areas (at all points in travel) are always to be used.

• Have your teen develop a short list of her safety rules (without your input) and see how savvy she is on these issues.

• Read *Respecting the Gift* by Gavin de Becker, a securities expert who has written this terrific book on how to protect our kids. And teach your daughter to listen to her own body signals regarding safety and danger.

• Try finding another working parent, perhaps the mother of one of your daughter's friends, with a different schedule than yours, and swap girl dates to cover some of the after-school time at a friend's house.

—Karen L. Maudlin, *Christian Parenting Today*, Winter 2004

Q: I feel like I'm always disciplining my kids and yet never seem to get anywhere. I punish them for back talk and remind them to be thoughtful. Am I too strict or too lenient? Everybody seems to have a different theory on discipline. I feel like such a failure.

A: I've discovered it helps to recognize two prevalent philosophies that shape disciplining styles—and how they differ.

1. *The religion of self-esteem* teaches that our most important job as a parent is to make our child feel good about himself, to be secure, even to like us. Someone who follows this style tends to be lenient in disciplining. This approach to discipline is tempting, especially if you come from an abusive or legalistic background. But keep in mind that love and discipline aren't opposites; they're inseparable partners. You build a child's sense of self-esteem when he knows the boundaries.

2. *The religion of regulations* teaches that to make your child behave, you must have long lists of rules. But it's easy to overburden children with so many expectations that they begin to feel as though they'll never measure up. When you do this to your children, they become frustrated and insecure.

Most of us tend either toward disciplining according to the religion of self-esteem or the religion of regulations. So recognize your tendency and take steps to balance your style. Keep in mind the ultimate goal of discipline, which is to train your children to obey you, the one who loves them, so that as they grow, they'll be better able to obey God.

—Susan Alexander Yates, *Today's Christian Woman*, September/October 2000

How to Avoid Lopsided Discipline

1. To avoid becoming too permissive:

Be firm during your child's early years, then loosen up as he gets older. Doing the opposite usually backfires. Your young child must learn that when you say "no," you mean "no," not "maybe"—even if he pitches a temper tantrum.

Don't be afraid to expect your child to behave, and provide consequences if he doesn't. Be sure to follow through with punishment. Kids need structure, and if you threaten your child but don't follow through when he misbehaves, he learns his actions don't have consequences. This devalues him, which is just the opposite of what you want to accomplish.

Teach your child to wait. That toddler who wants a cookie right before dinner must be taught to wait until after he finishes his dinner. The child who wants to hang out with her friends has to learn to wait until she has finished her chores. Much of life involves waiting, and you do your children a disservice if you don't teach them the art of delayed gratification. If they learn this lesson while they're young, they're more likely as teens to wait for sex until they're married.

Don't be manipulated by feelings. Validate your child's feelings—they're real. But then teach your child to do what is right, even if she doesn't feel like it. God uses tough times as life preparation. A mature person does what's right, not necessarily what she feels like doing.

2. To avoid becoming too rigid:

Be consistent in enforcing crucial regulations. It's far better to have a few rules you consistently enforce than a long list you don't. Determine what you expect and what the consequences are for infractions. Then follow through.

Make sure the punishment is realistic. It needs to fit the infraction. Don't say to your young child, "Since you didn't finish your breakfast, you can't have anything to eat for the rest of the day." Instead say, "No sweets or snacks until you eat a healthy meal."

Give lots of praise. It's easy to praise your child for earning an A or making the winning goal. But the bulk of your praise should be for her character. Kids come into the world with varying levels of ability, but all children can grow. So say, "Sweetie, I'm proud of the way you've befriended Janet. You have the gift of kindness. I'm proud of you."

Have fun as a family. Laugh and do crazy things. Go out for ice cream in the middle of the night. Play hide-and-seek in the dark. Move the furniture out of a room, put on some old music, and dance.

Collect jokes and read them at the dinner table. Make your home fun.

—Susan Alexander Yates, *Today's Christian Woman*, September/October 2000

Q: My eight-year-old son was recently diagnosed by a Christian psychologist as having ADHD (Attention Deficit Hyperactivity Disorder), and he recommended Ritalin. Does God really want us to change our children's behavior through medication?

A: First, I commend you for taking your son in for a psychological assessment, which should have included ADHD questionnaires for parents, teachers, and others, a computerized attention test, and a clinical interview to ascertain the pattern, intensity, frequency, and duration of the attention problem. Many parents don't know where to get these tests done, or they don't understand the benefits of professional testing. (Go to www.ADD.org for a list of professionals in your area.)

If your child was diabetic, you would not withhold insulin from him. I believe the same principle applies here. Your son has a problem that can be treated with medication. If you trust the psychologist and believe that your son's behavior cannot be managed without Ritalin, then you can feel justified in using medication. In addition to medication, I recommend four to six sessions with an ADHD specialist on impulse control to help your son begin a good school experience.

While our children are created in the image of God, it is unwise to see them—or ourselves—as finished products. It seems your son needs help controlling his impulses and energy, not only for his benefit, but also for the benefit of others. If you have committed this matter to prayer, believe that you have been given wise counsel from the psychologist, and see Ritalin as an aid to help your son manage his behavior, you can trust that God will honor your decision.

—Karen L. Maudlin, *Christian Parenting Today*, September/October 2001

Q: My three kids just can't get along! What can I do to stop the constant teasing, tattling, and fighting?

A: I can offer two thoughts: one that's helped my kids, and one that helps me.

First, I've come to realize that 90 percent of what my kids argue about is stupid stuff that doesn't even matter to them. What matters to them is fighting about it. With that in mind, I've found it helps simply to try to make them laugh and then *just let it go* (my daily mantra).

For example, one day my girls were bickering about something silly, so I interrupted them and announced, "All that squabbling is not music to my ears. So I want you both to go into the bathroom and don't come out until you've put your disagreement to music."

They thought I'd lost my marbles. But I insisted, and within five minutes they were giggling behind closed doors. After fifteen minutes, they were in the kitchen performing their song, complete with hand motions. As you can guess, the disagreement was forgotten.

But the thing that's helped me the most with sibling rivalry has been an attitude adjustment—mine! I once heard a Christian radio-show guest explain that the family is a microcosm of all relationships. I realized relationships are some of the hardest things to deal with. So every time my children fight with each other, speak unkindly, or treat my authority with disrespect, I have an opportunity to teach them how to navigate future relationships. What a privilege God has given me as a parent.

—Lisa Welchel, *Christian Parenting Today*, Spring 2005

Q: How do I stay connected to my twelve-year-old son as he moves into his teenage years?

A: In my experience, twelve-year-old-boys are the tightest-lipped creatures on the planet. Still, there are plenty of great ways to stay close to your son as he enters this new stage of life:

Get active. Boys are typically doers more than talkers. Think of a sport, game, or hobby that the two of you can do together, perhaps with another mother and son. Plan a regular date with your son and give him some input on what you can do together.

Use technology. If you work outside the home, instant message (IM) your son when you know he'll be online after school. Send him an e-mail to let him know you're excited to see him when you get home. Even if you're there when he gets the message, he'll know you've been thinking of him.

Check in every day. One way or another, make the time to ask your teen how his day went, share highlights about yours, and follow up on his activities and friends.

Offer a hangout. The more you can be the host place for his friends, the more you'll know about his friends, his interests, and his life.

Meet the girls in his life. Young teen girls are much more talkative than their male counterparts, so you'll get more insight into his life from his female buddies than you're likely to get from him.

—Karen L. Maudlin, *Christian Parenting Today*, Spring 2004

Q: How can I stop my child from arguing every time I ask her to do something?

A: If you wanted your child to learn to play the piano, you'd find her a good piano teacher. Between lessons, your child would practice her new skills. With continued instruction and practice, her skills would gradually improve. This is the same with good discipline. When we want our children to learn a new behavioral skill, we need to teach it to them and then follow up with lots of opportunities to practice.

For example, you want your daughter to be a better listener—to respond quickly and respectfully, not slowly and grudgingly. Sit down together and explain the Fast Listening plan. Keep it simple. Then, spend a few minutes practicing the plan together through role-play. For example, pretend that you're asking your child to turn off the TV, and let her practice saying, "Okay, Mom," and turning the TV off. Give her a big hug and tell her she did an awesome job. Then pretend you're asking her to pick up a couple toys, and so on. Spend about five minutes practicing three or four times a week. Make sure the practices are fun, fast-paced, and filled with positive attention.

—Todd Cartmell, *Christian Parenting Today*, Winter 2005

Q: I recently caught my six-year-old son and a seven-year-old girl showing each other their private parts. How do I explain the severity of their actions without blowing it out of proportion?

A: Unless there was inappropriate touching involved in this incident, there is likely no sexual intent in their curiosity. It is normal for kids your son's age to explore their bodies in nonsexual ways. Now that the door has been opened, you can use this as an opportunity to start talking to your son about his body. This is not the time to talk about sex, but rather a first step in helping your son discover why his body is special. In doing so, you are paving the way for more detailed conversations down the road.

For now, you might say something such as, "God made our bodies and they are beautiful in all parts. However, the private parts are special, so we keep them covered up when we're with other people. Sometimes parents and doctors need to see our private parts to make sure they are healthy. But other than that, there's no need for anyone to look at your private parts right now. I know you didn't know this when you and Susie were together, but from now on it's important to keep your private parts covered and not show others." Give your son a chance to ask questions and answer them honestly. Then pray together, giving thanks for your son's body and asking Jesus to help him take good care of it.

—Karen L. Maudlin, *Christian Parenting Today*, Fall 2004

Q: How do I explain to my child that his father's pornography addiction is the primary reason for our marital separation?

A: When a father drinks or is physically abusive, the effects of his problem are painfully obvious even to children who often are both angry and relieved when their parents separate. But hidden issues like pornography and homosexuality can be incomprehensible to them. A counselor can suggest questions your boy may ask and help you with your responses. Inevitably your son will wonder why his daddy needs to go.

Tell your son as much of the truth as you can without placing value judgments on his father's behavior. Instead of exclaiming, "Your daddy is a creep," you'd be wiser to say, "Daddy has made some bad choices. He's done some things that are not OK." Identifying the problem as pornography or homosexuality will depend on the age and maturity of your child. Answer only the question your child asks. If he has a follow-up question, answer it. Don't over-answer the question.

Today's children are less innocent than they used to be. Don't underestimate what they're capable of understanding. If the child hints at the question he really wants to ask, be an active listener and answer him. Tell him, "If you have any questions today or any time, please ask." Be prepared for him to ask verbally or through his actions if this was his fault, and let him know the problem has nothing to do with him.

The most important thing you can provide your child is assurance. "We love you. It's OK to feel sad. We can talk about this again. We will always love you!"

—Marlene LeFever, with the help of Dr. Jim Oraker and Chaplain May Hertel,
Christian Parenting Today, Spring 2005

Q: How do I nurture my children's dreams and help them follow God's plans for their lives?

A: The first step is to know your children uniquely and individually. Make an effort to learn their personality bents, their interests, and their yearnings. Listen, really listen, even when you are tired or distracted. Foster their dreams with these ideas:

1. Take weekly trips to the library. Plan on being there for at least an hour so your children can meander and dawdle. They need time to discover their interests.

2. Read together as a family whenever you can. This type of interaction promotes wonderful discussions.

3. Start thinking seriously about college when your children reach ninth grade. You don't have to make decisions yet, but the more research you do, the more opportunities for learning (and financing that learning) you'll discover.

4. Work closely with your children's school guidance counselors. These counselors have a wealth of information to share.

5. Commit your children's dreams to the Lord. As Psalm 37:5 says, "Commit your way to the LORD; trust in him and he will do this" (NIV).

Our children's dreams often seem out of reach. But through our words, our faith, and our example, we can assure them that God's plans for them will exceed anything they can imagine.

—Barbara Schiller, *Christian Parenting Today*, May/June 2000

Q: My fifteen-year-old daughter is starting to doubt God's existence. What can I do?

A: Doubt is a normal part of Christian life, especially for teens. A child who wrestles with questions of faith now will likely develop a deeply rooted belief that will last for a lifetime. As your daughter works through her doubts, be sure to let her know that you are there to help her find answers to her toughest questions. I also recommend the following guidelines:

Ask open-ended questions. Find out what it is about Christianity that concerns her. Listen to her and ask follow-up questions.

Offer to help with research. When your daughter has a question you can't answer, tell her that you can both do some further exploration and come back in a week or two to review what you've each discovered. Encourage her to talk with Christian adults you both respect.

Review the past. Ask her what she thinks about her early childhood faith now. Use "I" statements to tell her about specific memories you have of her experiencing God's presence as a child. You might say, "I remember how you loved to pray for your friends." Don't be put off by what she says about her past.

Be patient. Your daughter may be at this stage for a long time. She may even reach a point where she says she doesn't believe in God anymore. As heartbreaking as that would be for you, stay connected to your daughter by continuing to model God's unconditional love for her.

Pray, pray, pray. One of our strongest callings as parents is to be prayer warriors for our children rather than worry warriors.

—Karen L. Maudlin, *Christian Parenting Today*, March/April 2002

Q: Our twelve-year-old likes a boy at her school and wants to "go" with him. It seems going together is really just a term her friends use for two people who like each other—our daughter isn't really interested in dating this boy. Is it all right to let our daughter do this?

A: For many first-time parents of tweeners, it's surprising just how quickly the boy-girl stuff comes along. But relax and take courage; follow the instincts God has placed in you, and consider these ideas for setting up your family dating strategy.

1. Learn the lingo. *Going together* at twelve does not mean the same thing as it does at fifteen or sixteen. At twelve, it usually means that a boy and a girl like each other. They may not have declared that they like each other but they might e-mail and IM (instant message) each other on the Internet, look at each other and smile in the halls at school. Ask your daughter what going together means in her school.

2. Decide at what age your daughter can:

> E-mail or IM a boy.
>
> Phone a boy or receive phone calls from one. Include time limits and cutoffs so these calls do not intrude on family time.
>
> Go out on group activities with and without supervision.
>
> Have after-school dates in public places.
>
> Spend time at a boy's house or invite him to her house (with parental supervision).
>
> Go on an official date with defined parameters on transportation, activities, and curfew.

—Karen L. Maudlin, *Christian Parenting Today*, Fall 2003

Q: With all of the education choices available today, how do I know what will be the best place for my child to learn?

A: The best first step you can take in choosing the right kind of school—whether public, private, or home—is to pray about the decision. At the same time, become a student of your child. How would you describe his or her learning style? Does he enjoy hearing stories or singing songs? The answers can become excellent clues as to whether or not your child will thrive in a particular school.

When our sons were in elementary school, we started out in the public school system but quickly became disenchanted after we heard different teachers make several comments that were diametrically opposed to our beliefs. At this juncture, it became critical to us to place our children in a private Christian school. Although this decision required a financial sacrifice, we felt the lifelong base of Christian teaching they'd be receiving outweighed the cost.

Several years later we moved from this city and took a year off to travel. Homeschooling became the perfect solution for our mobile lifestyle. When we finally settled into a new home in a new town, there were fewer choices for good private schools. We opted for the public school system based on its strong academic record. Two of our kids struggled in the public high school, though, so again homeschooling became the solution. Our other two sons continue to thrive in the public schools.

Every child is unique, and what suits one student won't be optimum for another.

—Marian V. Liautaud, *Parenting Connection* newsletter, Christianity Today International, February 2007

Q: My daughter was stung by a bee. Although she had a normal reaction to it physically, she is now terrified to the point of tears whenever she sees a bee or any flying insect. How can I help her get past this irrational fear?

A: Whether your child is dealing with an overwhelming fear of bees or some other fear-inducing issue, here are some ways to help her work through this problem:

• Start by validating your daughter's fear without catering to it. Let her know that you are concerned about her fear and that you want to help her get rid of it.

• Teach your daughter positive coping statements, such as, "I can deal with bees and get over my fear of them." She can say this to herself whenever she's in a situation where she feels her fear coming on.

• Identify her negative perceptions and challenge them. In her mind, the original incident might have seemed worse than it really was. Have her talk through what really happened and how she handled it.

• Ask her to recall times when she overcame something she didn't think she could. Maybe she mastered a difficult math concept or scored a soccer goal. Remind her that she can overcome this fear of bees as well.

• Reward all her attempts to overcome her fear with plenty of praise. When she has a setback, let her know that's normal.

—Karen L. Maudlin, *Christian Parenting Today*, March/April 2002

Additional Resources

Books:

Surviving the Teenage Hormone Takeover: A Guide for Moms,
Nisha Jackson, Ph.D. (Thomas Nelson, 2006).

The Story of Me: God's Design for Sex, Stan and Brenna Jones, and Joel Spector
(NavPress, 2007), for sharing information about sex with small children

Grace Based Parenting: Set Your Family Free,
Tim Kimmel (Thomas Nelson, 2005).

*Talking to Your Kids About Sex: How to Have a lifetime of Age-Appropriate Conversations with
Your Children About Healthy Sexuality,* Mark Laaser (WaterBrook, 1997)

The Smart Stepfamily: Seven Steps to a Healthy Family,
Ron L. Deal (Bethany House, 2006)

A Positive Plan for Creating More Fun, Less Whining,
Karol Ladd (Thomas Nelson, 2006).

Help Your Twenty Somethings Get a Life . . . and Get It Now,
Ross Campbell, M.D. (Thomas Nelson, 2007).

Internet Protect Your Kids: Keep Your Children Safe from the Dark Side of Technology,
Stephen Arterburn and Roger Marsh (Thomas Nelson, 2007).

Websites:

www.singleparentfamilyresources.com
Help for single parents

www.successfulstepfamilies.com
Help for stepparenting

www.fotf.org
Focus on the Family resources for family issues and concerns

Questions About

Family

Q: My husband and I have been married five years and have a three-year-old son. My husband also has a twelve-year-old daughter from a previous marriage. I feel as though I'm on the outside looking in when it comes to his daughter. When she stays with us, she's belligerent and disrespectful to me. Sometimes my husband favors his daughter over me—or at least doesn't stand up for me. Help!

A: Let's begin by thinking about what it's like to be your stepdaughter.

First, she can't have what she most wants in a family; her mom and dad under the same roof, happily married. You, more than anyone else, remind her of that loss. You're with her father, and he loves you, not her mother.

At age twelve, your stepdaughter probably doesn't know what to do with her confusion, grief, and anger. She may want you on the outside looking in when it comes to her relationship with her dad. If she can't have her mom there, she doesn't want you taking her place.

She also may be angry with her dad and be taking it out on you to preserve her relationship with him. Your stepdaughter may fear being preempted by you and your son, so she fights to exclude you.

Try not to take her reactions personally. It may be years before she's secure enough to have a good relationship with you.

Talk to your husband about her disrespect and belligerence. He needs to help his daughter find more appropriate ways to express her negative feelings. Anger and sadness don't give her the right to be disrespectful.

—Diane Mandt Langberg, *Today's Christian Woman*, March/April 2003

FAMILY

Q: I want to cultivate a close relationship with my grandchildren. The problem is that half of them live across the country, and the ones who live nearby are school age and are constantly tied up with sports activities. What are some ways I can grow close to these grandkids in spite of the miles and the busyness?

A: Today, the Internet makes daily communication easy and allows you to send pictures, e-cards, educational articles, and much more. Christian bookstores are stocked with children's videos, praise CDs, character-building stories, and activity books for all ages. Some next-day shipping companies will pick up packages right at your doorstep.

Ask your children what the grandchildren get excited about and brainstorm with them with those ideas in mind. Find out if your grandchildren have reading goals at school. If they do, you might want to contribute a book for that project. For your grandchildren nearby, offer to provide homework relief for their parents. If you have taken an especially interesting trip, have a pet, or enjoy a special hobby such as gardening, send your grandchildren pictures in a small album so they can share in your life, too.

Whatever you decide to do to cultivate closeness with your grandchildren, there's nothing more special than that personal phone call. Hearing Grandma or Grandpa's voice may be just what a child needs on that particular day.

—Gail Gallagher, *Christian Parenting Today*, Winter 2000

Q: My sister-in-law drives me crazy. She's negative and opinionated. I don't want to harp on my husband's family, but I'm having a hard time with my attitude. Are there ways I can learn to accept her?

A: You and your sister-in-law may never become best friends, but here are some strategies to help you accept her.

1. *Find neutral territory.* If you're a neat freak and your sister-in-law isn't, she may be uncomfortable hanging out at your house. Try meeting at a restaurant or somewhere that you'll both enjoy, such as a museum exhibit.

2. *Work hard to be a friend.* Try treating her like any other new friend; spend time with her one-on-one, getting to know her. Pay attention to the little clues she gives you about her life.

3. *Look for common ground.* When you're so different from your husband's sibling, it may be hard to find anything in common. But the search is worth the effort.

4. *Don't expect her to be like your husband.* Just because they're siblings doesn't mean brother and sister are alike. It might help to sit down and list your sister-in-law's good qualities, then refer to them frequently as a reminder.

5. *Allow each other to change.* The woman you first know as your sister-in-law will change and grow over time, just like you. As she feels more comfortable sharing her life with you, focus on just listening. She'll be much more likely to open up to you and to listen to what you have to say.

—Maria Lopez, *Today's Christian Woman*, July/August 2003

Q: When my husband, a widower, and I married, we became an instant family with his two children from a previous marriage. It's been tough to get his kids to accept me. How can I win over my stepchildren?

A: Winning over your stepchildren may be a legitimate goal, but it shouldn't be your immediate objective. It's important to remember that for children living in a blended family, the rules have suddenly changed. Having a stepmother was not the children's choice. You need to give children plenty of time and emotional breathing space to adjust to a new family.

As you think about your role as a stepmother, it may help to refocus your goal. Rather than asking, "How do I want to love these children?" you might try asking, "How do these children want to be loved?" Discovering the answer to that means understanding the children's needs, observing them, and entering into their world as they permit.

Try to defuse any competition with the other mother, and search for ways to affirm the good and unique things she did. Don't put the stepchildren in a defensive posture where they feel the need to prove their first mom was best.

Stepchildren also need to continue feeling as if their dad is on their team. That may mean being more discreet at home and in public with your displays of affection toward your husband. Look at stepparenting as a chance to step into the shoes of your stepchildren. The more you try to look at things from the child's point of view, the greater will be your incentive to move cautiously and carefully into a rewarding parenting experience.

—Gail MacDonald, *Parenting: Questions Women Ask* (Multnomah, 1992)

Q: My husband's extended family lives far away from us. What are some ways I can help my kids know this part of their family and stay connected in spite of the miles that separate us?

A: With extended family so scattered and our lives so busy, how can we bring back the feelings that come from being part of a close-knit clan? Here are a few ideas that might help tighten your family circle.

1. *An Extended Family Album.* Gather as many family photos as you can find, place them in an album, and identify each person by name and relation (e.g. Mary Smith, second cousin). That will acquaint your children with some rarely seen faces and will provide them with a sense of belonging to a larger unit.

2. *The Digital Connection.* The Internet provides several great ways to stay connected across the miles. My friend Michele set up her own website for her across-the-country crew. She included pictures of her girls, news from her home, and even a guest book so she could see who had visited the site. She could then forward them a personal note.

3. *Round Robin Letters.* Several years ago, when my sisters and I lived in separate states, we felt disconnected. Having always been close, we wanted to know more about what was going on in each other's daily life, so we initiated a round robin letter. One sister wrote about what was happening in her household, then mailed her note to me. I added my own letter, put it with hers, and sent them both off to my other sister. She, in turn, included a letter and sent the whole bunch back to the first sister. After the first sister

replaced her original note with an update, she sent the letters off for a new round. The round robin letters helped us to feel in touch again.

4. *Have a Reunion.* Probably the best way to keep family ties is to spend time together. And what better way to do this than the tried-and-true family reunion? Planning a reunion can be daunting, so some never get off the ground. But remember, a reunion can be as complex or simple as the family chooses to make it. Some families hold huge blow-out reunions, hosting a hundred or more distant relatives. A smaller, less hectic reunion can be just as rewarding. Be sure, however, to begin organizing early and notify the guests far in advance of your target date. Most people need time to make plans and won't be able to attend if you let them know the week before. If you plan to make it an annual event, holding it at the same time each year makes scheduling easy for everyone.

5. *The Cousin Camp.* If spending a week with your family sounds great, but the adults can't seem to synchronize time off, have a Cousin Camp. It's the latest thing for acquainting the kids with kinfolk. As adults and their families scatter, faraway cousins might see each other only during visits to their grandparents' home, which are often on hectic holidays. To give the kids more opportunities to get to know each other, many grandparents now are hosting Cousin Camps at a less stressful time.

—Beverly Dillard, *Today's Christian Woman*, March/April 2004

Q: Each member of my family is involved in multiple activities throughout the week. We've fallen into grab-it-and-run family dinners. I know things have to change. How do we reclaim family mealtime?

A: Here are some suggestions for recapturing the art of family meals:

Decide to be together certain nights each week—then do it. Begin with one or two nights if necessary. You and your husband should agree on this policy before talking to your kids. Be willing to stand firm when different family members protest.

Turn off the phone. Don't answer the phone during mealtime, and teach your kids not to phone others during the meal.

Prepare the meal or clean up together. The art of merely enjoying each other's company is lost if we feel awkward simply sitting and visiting. But when family members work together on a project, good conversations often take place naturally, without having a specific agenda to discuss.

Eat at the table facing each other. Sitting at a counter, while convenient at times, doesn't encourage interaction among family members. It's hard to talk to someone you can't see clearly. So face each other. And turn the television off during the meal.

Have everyone come at the same time and remain at the table until everyone is excused. One way to make sure your kids remain at the table is to end each meal with a closing prayer or a short devotion.

—Susan Alexander Yates, *Today's Christian Woman*, November/December 1996

FAMILY

Good Conversation Starters for Family Meals

Here are some guidelines for getting your family
to talk about their day over dinner:

1. No one is allowed to pass;
everyone is required to share something.

2. Don't be in a hurry. No rushing.

3. Nothing is too mundane.

4. Ask follow-up questions such as:
who, what, where, when, why?

5. No judgments or disciplining at the table. You can't say,
"Well, that was a stupid thing to do"
or "I don't know why you said that to them."

6. No "fixing." This is just the time to listen and
learn about the other person.

—Randy Frazee, *Making Room for Life* (Zondervan, 2003)

FAMILY

Q: My husband and I each brought children from previous marriages into our second marriage. What's it going to take to actually become a blended family?

A: Experts say it typically takes four to eight years for a new family to blend, or to feel like a real family rather than a stepfamily. But of the second marriages that fail, most do so in the first four years before families realistically could be expected to blend.

For you to significantly improve your marriage's survival rate, put your marriage before the kids. The single most destructive thing a husband or wife can do in a second marriage is to side with their biological child against the spouse. Conquer those biological tendencies and you'll build your marriage. That's the greatest thing you can do for kids who have been through the intense pain of seeing their previous family disintegrate.

Finding a church with a strong blended-family ministry is also critical. It can point you toward counseling, toward a mentor couple, or toward small groups where blended-family couples hash out tough questions together.

—Jim Killam, *Marriage Partnership*, Spring 2004

Q: My husband and I have been married for two years, and we have a seventeen-month-old as well as two children from my previous marriage. He's great with the baby because they can just play together, but he's quick to say no when the older kids ask for something. He expects too much from them for their ages and picks on them when they don't measure up. My children are losing the affection they used to have for him. How can I talk to my husband about this?

A: A meaningful conversation with your husband could be the beginning of a solution. But he will likely feel defensive when you talk to him about this, so you'll need to think very carefully about what you want to talk about.

What do your older children want their relationship with their stepfather to be like? I'd suggest talking one-on-one with each child to find out what they think could help the relationship grow.

Write down their responses and share them with your husband when you talk with him. (Reframe the requests if they are too negative). Let him know the changes you've seen in your children, and tell him that you want to tackle the problem together.

Your husband may never parent exactly like you do. Do your best to let him express love in his own unique ways as long as they are not harmful to your children.

Finally, encourage your husband to spend time doing something fun with each of your older children. The more time he spends getting to know them, the more he'll understand what they need from him as a stepfather.

—Karen L. Maudlin, *Christian Parenting Today*, Spring 2003

The Stepparent Trap

Many couples in second marriages find the problem isn't their spouse; it's the children. One woman said, "I love my husband; I wish I could divorce his kids." Trying to parent those children can bring intense conflict to the entire family. So what should you know and do?

Realize:

- Stepfamilies (blended families) are born of loss. That's not always easy for the remarried couple to remember, but the children don't forget.

- Stepparents and stepchildren do not necessarily love each other. Usually there is another biological parent who influences the family.

- Because the parent-child bond existed before the couple bond, the child may feel pushed out of a special relationship with the biological parent and may fight the growth of intimacy between the new spouses.

- Problems may flow from unexpressed expectations based on an assumption that a new family will be created.

- Stepfamilies must respect their distinctive pasts, understand them, and try to blend them. But the biological parent and children need to celebrate some of their past separately.

- Conflicts over discipline can be huge. The blending spouse's parental values may differ. Spouses must talk as spouses, but parents must talk as parents. So when you have an issue with your spouse's parenting tactics, talk in private, saying something like, "I love you, but when I hear you speak to my son, Johnny, in harsh tones, I lose respect for you. I don't appreciate your doing that."

What to Do:

• Pray over every aspect of your new family—expectations, boundaries, parenting conflicts.

• Find a safe support network where you can discuss problems and receive input. You may try looking in your church to start.

• Never put down the former spouse in the child's presence. When that happens, you dishonor the child's source of life.

• Try to put yourself in that child's place; think about the difficulty he or she may be going through. Remember, the child didn't ask for the divorce or the parent's death.

• Respect and guard parental boundaries. Avoid parenting the stepchild; allow that to be done strictly by the biological parent. Obviously there may be times when younger children require immediate parenting, which you may have to do if the biological parent isn't available. But, even those times should be kept to a minimum.

• Keep a united front. Avoid criticizing or contradicting your spouse in front of the children.

• Make marriage your top priority. The best thing for your children is to see a strong marriage. They've experienced one family's disintegration; don't allow them to experience another.

—Scottie May, from *Marriage Partnership*, Spring 2004

Q: When my husband and I envisioned retirement, we pictured white sandy beaches or a beautiful retirement village. Instead, we've made a complete U-turn: We're raising our granddaughter! I feel good about the decision we've made to parent her, but sometimes I feel disappointed that the retirement years aren't what I thought they'd be. How can I have a better attitude?

A: Many of today's grandparents are abandoning their retirement dreams and returning to the world of report cards, temper tantrums, and sleepovers. When grandparents take on the role of parent to their grandchildren, they know that there are many unseen challenges to face.

Amanda is a single woman in her forties whose adult daughter is on drugs. Amanda didn't hesitate to rescue her granddaughter from a potentially dangerous situation. She has had her granddaughter for two years and they make quite a team. Amanda's seven-year-old granddaughter has been richly blessed and saved from a life of trouble. Amanda, who has MS and is in a wheelchair, has a loving companion and a great helper. Amanda had all kinds of valid reasons to say no to taking in her granddaughter, yet she chose to do what she felt God was asking her to do.

There are countless stories of grandparents of all ages who are making U-turns and caring for their grandchildren in difficult circumstances. It can often feel discouraging. But remember that no matter how impossible a problem looks, there is a solution rooted in our heavenly Father.

—Gail Gallagher, *Christian Parenting Today*, Spring 2003

Additional Resources

Books:

Making Room for Life: Trading Chaotic Lifestyles for Connected Relationships,
Randy Frazee (Zondervan, 2003).

Treasures of a Grandmother's Heart: Finding Pearls of Wisdom in Everyday Moments,
Esther Burroughs (New Hope Publishers, 2002).

Step-Parenting 101,
Dr. Kevin Leman (Thomas Nelson, 2007).

The Fulfilled Family: God's Design for Your Home,
John MacArthur (Thomas Nelson, 2005).

The Most Important Place on Earth: What a Christian Home Looks Like and How to Build One,
Robert Wolgemuth (Thomas Nelson, 2006).

Websites:

www.myfamily.com
Family website

www.family-reunion.com
Reunion planning

www.singleparentfamilyresources.com
Single parenting

www.fotf.org
Focus on the Family provides resources for family issues and concerns

www.chhs.gsu.edu
National Center on Grandparents Raising Children

FAMILY

Questions About

Spiritual Growth

Q: I know I should be reading my Bible, but I don't really want to. How can I develop a desire for God's Word?

A: If you want to develop a consistent desire for Scripture, here are five things you can do:

1. *Remember the Bible's benefits.* Just as satisfying physical craving releases feel-good chemicals in our brains, satisfying a hunger for Scripture releases spiritual benefits and blessings in our lives, such as increased wisdom, comfort, and peace.

2. *Ask God to give you the desire for His Word.* Each day, ask God to give you a deep-rooted desire to spend time reading and studying the Bible. Then be alert for those inner promptings.

3. *Make daily Bible reading a habit.* Experts say it takes twenty-one days to develop a habit. Decide on a reading or study plan and commit yourself to spending time in God's Word every day, whether you feel like it or not.

4. *Keep a spiritual journal.* Keep a record of how Scripture has affected your life. Take note of how various Scripture passages have touched your heart, motivated change in your life, or given you insight into life's circumstances.

5. *Customize your Bible study to fit your circumstances.* A mother of three preschoolers might not be able to devote the same amount of time and energy to reading God's Word as a woman whose children are in school. Finding the method of study and reading that works for where you are right now will keep you from giving up in frustration.

—Katrina Baker, *Today's Christian Woman*, July/August 2004

Q: How can journaling help me grow spiritually?

A: Journaling can be an amazing tool to help you record God's transforming work in your heart. There are so many ways you can chronicle your faith walk.

You can collect quotes and thought-provoking observations from your favorite Christian writers. A Quotes Journal is a wonderful way for you to meditate on some of the amazing things you're learning in your spiritual walk.

Journals are the perfect place to record your big prayer requests. Jot down some seemingly impossible requests in your journal, then watch and record the amazing ways God answers each prayer.

If you enjoy the beauty of God's creation, enjoy His handiwork further by keeping a Creator's Journal. Find pictures that express all kinds of natural elements, press leaves and flowers, or shoot photos reminding you of different seasons and types of weather. Under each illustration, write down reasons why these scenes inspire you. You also can incorporate Scripture that speaks about God's workmanship.

Whether you want to expand your prayer life, express your admiration of creation, give thanks, boost your faith, or trace God's work in the lives of your loved ones, there's a journaling style for you.

—Jody Veenker, *Today's Christian Woman*, May/June 2004

Q: My life is so busy. How can I find time to pray?

A: My prayer life underwent a radical transformation when I discovered the apostle Paul's command to pray continually (1 Thess. 5:17). That means more than just spending a lot of time in prayer; it means having a continual dialogue with God wherever I go. Whether you're married or single, with or without children, here's how to begin building a 24/7 prayer life.

1. *Get a good start.* For me, a life of continuous prayer starts even before I lift my head off the pillow. I say, "Lord, this is the day that You have made; help me focus on You in the midst of all I've got to do."

I read God's Word before the demands of the day flood in, because Scripture never fails to draw me into prayer and praise. Praying things such as "Lord, help me to trust in You with all my heart and not lean on my own understanding" (Prov. 3:5–6), or "Thank You, Father, that You are compassionate and gracious, slow to anger and abounding in love" (Ps. 103:8), helps me zero in on the Mountain Mover instead of the mountains I may be facing.

2. *Clue into visual reminders.* I use things around me as visual cues to prompt me to pray. For example, as I pass the windows of neighbors' houses on my morning walk, I pray, "God, let Your light shine in; bless them and draw them closer so they'll know You." With visual cues to prompt you, all your daily activities—gardening, cleaning, working, or creating—become springboards to conversation with God.

3. *Use tools to stay focused.* It's easy for my mind to wander during prayer. One way I counteract this is by using the acronym B-L-E-S-S as I pray for

my family and friends. Each letter in the acronym stands for a key area of life: Body, Labor, Emotions, Social Life, and Spirituality.

For example, for our son, Chris, who is now a Navy doctor, I prayed today: "Lord, bless Chris' *body*; strengthen and protect him during his deployment. Bless Chris' *labor*; give him wisdom as he cares for the Marines' medical needs and injuries. Bless Chris' *emotional* life; and so on.

4. *Pray on the spot.* If a friend asks me to pray for a specific need, I offer to pray with her right then. If a speeding ambulance passes me while I'm driving, I immediately pray for the people in it and for the doctors who will care for the injured people at the hospital.

—Cheri Fuller, *Today's Christian Woman*, March/April 2004

Q: So many of my prayers seem superficial. How can I say the kind of prayers that move the heart of God?

A: Jesus says, "Ask and it will be given to you; seek and you will find; knock and the door will be opened to you. For everyone who asks receives; he who seeks finds; and to him who knocks, the door will be opened" (Matt. 7:7–8 NIV). But asking, seeking, and knocking aren't secret formulas for getting what we want from God; they're ways to get *more* of God. If you truly want to move God's heart, begin to practice prayer that seeks the Giver more than the gifts.

We ask God to heal physical ailments, provide safe travel, and to be with us. Of course God cares about these things. But prayer is spiritual work toward a spiritual end. God wants to rub off our rough edges and clean up our character. When our prayers move from the superficial to the significant, we invite God to do no less than a deep, transforming, igniting work in our lives and in the lives of those for whom we're praying.

Jesus warned: "When you pray, do not be like the hypocrites, for they love to pray standing in the synagogues and on the street corners to be seen by men. I tell you the truth, they have received their reward in full. But when you pray, go into your room, close the doors and pray to your Father, who is unseen. Then your Father, who sees what is done in secret, will reward you" (Matt. 6:5–6 NIV).

I can perform public prayers or make claims of private prayer and settle for the applause of people; or I can go to a secret place, shut the door, and commune with God. It's in that secret place with Him that you and I find our most blessed reward—not impressing others, but cultivating true intimacy with Him.

According to Hebrews 5:7–8, "During the days of Jesus' life on earth, he offered up prayers and petitions with loud cries and tears to the one who could save him from death, and he was heard because of his reverent submission. Although he was a son, he learned obedience from what he suffered" (NIV).

Submissive prayer is prayer that welcomes God to work in and through my suffering rather than begs Him to take it away. Submissive prayer is changing from someone who knew a lot about God into someone who experiences God in deep, though sometimes difficult, ways.

Our heavenly Father has no need for a show or secret formulas, and He's not interested in keeping things superficial. He loves it when we come to Him because He simply wants to talk with us.

—Nancy Guthrie, *Today's Christian Woman*, March/April 2006

Q: We recently left our church and are now trying to find a new place to worship. What is the best way to find a church home for my family?

A: According to the Barna Research Group, one in seven people will look for a new church this year. There are five important things to look for as you search for a new church.

1. *Does this church preach the right message?* Look for a place where truth is preached from the Bible; where God's Word is seen as living, relevant, changeless, and inerrant rather than just a good book filled with advice on how to be a more loving, moral person.

2. *Is this church a caring community?* We all want a church home where we feel welcome, a place where we belong.

3. *Does this church provide meaningful worship?* For all our style preferences, it's the message in the music that counts. Worship isn't simply about meeting a style preference or eliciting a purely emotional response within the worshiper; its purpose is to focus on and glorify God.

4. *Is the church convenient?* Your church needs to be a distance that's convenient enough for you to feel you have the opportunity to get plugged in, and to be an active member rather than just an attendee.

5. *Can you plug into this church's serving opportunities?* God gives you gifts and talents for use in building His church. But when you make a church change, you may temporarily be in limbo as you wait and watch for opportunities to serve your new community.

—Julie-Alyson Ieron, *Today's Christian Woman*, July/August 2005

SPIRITUAL GROWTH

Q: I desperately need a day of rest, but even Sundays are loaded with activities. How can I escape the pace of our culture and honor the Sabbath?

A: The word *Sabbath* literally means stop, pause, cease, desist. In the Ten Commandments, the Israelites are commanded to keep the Sabbath day holy, or separate, from the other weekdays. The marker of that holiness is the absence of work. One clear command about Sabbath-keeping forbids lighting a fire (Exod. 35:3). This mandate made clear that daughters, wives, and female servants wouldn't be expected to cook. All the food had to be prepared before the Sabbath began, and the dishes washed afterwards.

In our time, what's the equivalent of "lighting a fire"? What are those actions that send us into a work mode on Sunday? Turning on your computer, balancing the checkbook, weeding your garden, and cooking may put you into work mode. For others, gardening and cooking are relaxing, so these women would have a different list of work activities to avoid on the Sabbath.

Many women benefit from some silent time on the Sabbath. One mom with young children prepares a "Sabbath box" of special activities for her children. During one hour on Sunday afternoon, her children know they're expected to play alone, enjoying the delights in the Sabbath box while their parents get some silent time.

You'll receive many gifts from your commitment to honor the Sabbath. You'll receive a day free of multitasking. A day free of striving for perfection and productivity. A day to rest in God's goodness.

—Lynne M. Baab, *Today's Christian Woman*, September/October 2005

Q: I've been waiting for God's answer in a particular area of my life, but it feels like it's taking forever. What can I do to make the most of this waiting?

A: If you're going through a waiting period, here are three ways to profit from it:

1. *Wait quietly.* Today we live in the busiest, noisiest time in history. But God encourages His waiting ones to be still and spend time being quiet. In the Christian classic *Abundant Living*, author E. Stanley Jones says it's in spending quiet time with God that a Christian gains poise and power. Jones says, "One translator interprets the command, 'Be still, and know that I am God' this way: 'Be silent to God, and He will mold you.' Be silent to God, and He will make you the instrument of His purposes. [In silence] an all-wise Mind will brood over your mind, awakening it, stimulating it, and making it creative." God has a message in your wait, and in silence you can hear it clearly.

2. *Wait in hope.* Biblical hope isn't a wishy-washy, I-hope-this-will-turn-out-for-good-but-maybe-it-won't attitude. Biblical hope is the confident assurance that God is in charge, no matter what.

3. *Wait obediently.* The only waiting that is beneficial is obedient waiting, which takes place by aligning our actions as closely as we can with scriptural principles and asking God to adjust our attitude. As we wait on God, we must stay obedient. While you wait, live according to God's Word, seek Him, and meditate on His message.

—Faith Tibbetts McDonald, *Today's Christian Woman*, September/October 2002

Q: Most of my friends are Christians. How can I cultivate relationships with nonbelievers to reach them with the gospel?

A: First, *don't write people off.* Jesus reached out to people that everybody else gave up on—tax collectors, lepers, sinners, Gentiles. Think of your world. Is anyone so far from God that you see him or her as hopeless? Maybe it's someone in your extended family who ridicules your faith. Maybe it's somebody so deep in sin you think there's no chance of recovery. Don't ever say no to anyone when it comes to spreading the good news of the gospel. You never know when someone's heart will soften to the work of God's Spirit.

Next, be *the hands and feet of Jesus.* In Mark 1:40–45, a leper approached Jesus and begged to be made clean. The law said lepers couldn't have contact with non-lepers. But when this leper came to Jesus and asked, "Would you make me clean?" Jesus reached out to touch this man who hadn't been touched in years. Jesus didn't have to do that; He could have healed the man through the spoken word.

Was Jesus infected by leprosy? No, it was the other way around! Jesus was so full of life and health that He "infected" the leper with the good news of the kingdom of God. Jesus was more contagious with God's power and love than the leper was with his disease. If the Spirit of God lives inside you, you're like that. You can be a contagious Christian who infects others with God's power and love.

—John Ortberg, *Today's Christian Woman*, July/August 2002

Q: How can I keep pride from invading my life?

A: As Christians, we long to be righteous and victorious so we'll attract others to God. But when we start believing that our goodness comes from us instead of from Jesus Christ, that's when pride takes over. Here are six ways to help ward off this sneaky sin.

1. *Prayerfully analyze your motives.* Pride tells us we're something we're not—good. The truth is, we're all sinners in need of grace. So ask yourself, "Why am I doing this? Why am I so driven to do or be a certain thing? Is it to glorify God, or to make me look better?"

2. *Practice honoring others above yourself.* Proverbs 27:2 says, "Let another praise you, and not your own mouth" (NIV). This—in our competitive, self-promoting world—takes deliberate intention.

3. *Refuse to be judgmental.* We cannot know another's intent or motive. Jesus said, "Do not judge, or you too will be judged. For in the same way you judge others, you will be judged" (Matt. 7:1–2 NIV).

4. *Risk failure.* Pride says, "I must protect my image. I can't fail or look stupid; I must succeed." Humility says, "How I need your grace, God! I'll do my best, but the results are up to you."

5. *Learn to laugh at yourself.* The more seriously you take God, the less seriously you take yourself.

6. *Ask for help, advice, or prayer.* Listen to the opinions of others, and admit you may be wrong or that you don't have all the answers. When you're in need of prayer, ask for it.

—Nancie Carmichael, *Today's Christian Woman*, January/February 2005

Q: Are angels active in our world today?

A: The answer is yes, but the question makes me a bit nervous since our attitude toward angels often reflects a sentimental spirituality that isn't biblically accurate.

The Bible tells us a lot about angels. They don't marry or die (Luke 20:35–36). Angels are involved in revealing the law (Acts 7:38), bringing messages from God (Zech. 1:14–17), praising God (Heb. 1:6; Rev. 5:11–12), and protecting His people (Dan. 6:22; Acts 12:7–10).

Some angels rebelled against God (2 Pet. 2:4). Those angels, of whom Satan is chief, work through false teachers (2 Thess. 2:9–10; 1 Tim. 4:1–2), attempt to separate believers from God (Rom. 8:38–39), and tempt us to sin (1 Pet. 5:8).

But the Bible also teaches us about angels by what it doesn't say. We're never told to study angels or even to look actively for their appearance. Even in Hebrews 13:2, which says that by being hospitable some have unknowingly entertained angels, there is no admonition to be on the lookout for them. In Colossians 2:18–19, the apostle Paul warns us against giving angels undue attention.

Far from being models for sweet figurines, angels are powerful beings used by God to work in the world (Heb. 1:14). But the focus is never on them; it's on God and His work in our lives.

—Nancy Ortberg, *Today's Christian Woman*, November/December 2006

Additional Resources

Books:

Angels: God's Secret Agents,
Billy Graham (Thomas Nelson, 2000)

The One Year Book of Praying Through the Bible,
Cheri Fuller (Tyndale, 2003)

The One Year Book of Hope,
Nancy Guthrie (Tyndale, 2005)

Sabbath Keeping: Finding Freedom in the Rhythms of Rest,
Lynne M. Baab (InterVarsity, 2005)

If You Want to Walk on Water, You've Got to Get Out of the Boat,
John Ortberg (Zondervan, 2001)

A Daybook of Prayer: Meditations, Scriptures, and Prayers to Draw Near to the Heart of God
(Thomas Nelson, 2007)

Websites:

www.cherifuller.com
Contains a monthly column, resources, and inspiration on prayer by author Cheri Fuller

www.nanciecarmichael.com
Inspiration and encouragement for women

www.prayer-journal.com
Ideas and inspiration to help incorporate journaling into one's faith walk

Colleen Alden, a freelance writer, lives in North Carolina

Greg Askimakoupoulos, a freelance writer, lives in Mercer Island, Washington

Lynne M. Baab is author of *Sabbath Keeping: Finding Freedom in the Rhythms of Rest* (InterVarsity, 2005)

Katrina Baker, a freelance writer, lives near Pittsburgh, Pennsylvania

Carla Barnhill is the author of *Myth of the Perfect Mother* (Baker, 2004), and the former editor of *Christian Parenting Today* magazine. She is the mother of three and the wife of one (Jim). She and her family live in Minnesota.

Trisha Berg, contributing author to *Mom, You Make a Difference* (Revell, 2005) is a regular feature writer for *MOMSense Magazine*

Katherine G. Bond has written or contributed to more than twenty books, including *The Legend of the Valentine* (Zonderkidz, 2002). She lives in Duvall, Washington

Judith Briles, Luci Swindoll, and Mary Welchel. From *The Workplace: Questions Women Ask* (Christianity Today International, 1992)

Nancie Carmichael, author of *601 Quotes About Marriage and Family* (Tyndale, 1998), is former editor-at-large of *Virtue* magazine

Todd Cartmell a public speaker and child psychologist, is the author of *The Parent Survival Guide* (Zondervan, 2001). He has a clinical practice in Wheaton, Illinois

Amy Chapin is author of *365 Bible Promises for Hurting People* (Tyndale House, 1996)

Gary D. Chapman, is a marriage and relationship expert and best-selling author of *The Five Love Languages* (Moody, 1995) and *Covenant Marriage* (Broadman & Holman)

Patsy Clairmont is a speaker at Women of Faith conferences. She is the author of several books, including *God Uses Cracked Pots* (Focus on the Family, 1999), *Normal is Just a Setting on Your Dryer* (Tyndale House, 1999), and *Sportin' a 'Tude* (FOCUS, 1996). Her latest book is *Dancing Bones: Living Lively in the Valley* Thomas Nelson, 2007).

Judy Corey is the owner of the consulting company, Word and Spirit, in White Cloud, Michigan

Camerin Courtney, associate editor of *Today's Christian Woman*, is also a columnist for ChristianSinglesToday.com and writes movie reviews for ChristianityTodayMovies.com. She is author of two books: *Table for One* (Revell, 2002) and *The unGuide to Dating* (Revell, 2006).

Cindy Crosby is the author of *Waiting for Morning* (Baker, 2001), and is a regular contributor to *Today's Christian Woman*

Beverly Dillard is a freelance author living in Georgia

Christin Ditchfield is the host of the syndicated radio program "Take It to Heart!" She is a conference speaker and author of more than forty books, including *A Family Guide to Narnia* (Crossway Books, 2003)

T. Suzanne Eller is an inspirational speaker and author of *Real Teens, Real Stories, Real Life* (RiverOak, 2002), and is a regular contributor to *Today's Christian Woman*

Randy Frazee, author of *Making Room for Life* (Zondervan, 2003), is teaching pastor at Willow Creek Community Church, South Barrington, Illinois

Cheri Fuller is a speaker and author of several books, including *One Year of Praying Through the Bible* (Tyndale, 2003), and is a regular contributor to *Today's Christian Woman*

Gail Gallagher a freelance writer, is a former columnist for *Christian Parenting Today*

Dr. Tim A. Gardner, author of *Sacred Sex* (WaterBrook, 2002), is director of The Marriage Education and Policy Center at the Indiana Family Institute (an affiliate of Focus on the Family)

Verla Gillmor, president of LifeChasers, is a motivational speaker, executive coach, and author of *Reality Check, A Survival Manual for Christians in the Workplace* (Horizon Books, 2001), and is a regular contributor to *Today's Christian Woman*

Sheila Wray Gregoire is a syndicated parenting columnist, home-schooling mom, and author of four books, including *To Love, Honor and Vacuum: When you feel more like a maid than a wife and a mother* (Kregel Publications, 2003)

Gayle L. Gresham is a freelance writer living in Eastern Colorado

Nancy Guthrie is author of *Holding On to Hope: A Pathway Through Suffering to the Heart of God* (Tyndale, 2006)

Linda Hall is a mystery writer whose works include *The Josiah Files* (Thomas Nelson, 1993) and *November Veil (Bethel, 1996)*. She lives in Canada

Melissa Hambrick is a freelance writer living in Nashville, Tennessee.

Liz Curtis Higgs, humorist and storyteller, is author of *Bad Girls of the Bible* books, workbooks, and videos (Waterbrook, 1999), and is a regular contributor to *Today's Christian Woman*

Alicia Howe is a pseudonym for a writer and public relations specialist living in Florida

Al Hsu is an associate editor at InterVarsity Press. He is the author of *Singles at the Crossroads* (InterVarsity Press, 1997), *Grieving a Suicide* (InterVarsity Press, 2002), and *The Suburban Christian: Finding Spiritual Vitality in the Land of Plenty* (Intervarsity Press, 2006)

Kathi Hunter is a speaker and writer living in San Jose, California. She is a contributing writer to *Humor for a Woman's Heart* (Howard Books, 2002)

Julie-Allyson Ieron is author of several books, including *Courageous Women in the Bible* (Wesleyan Publishing House, 2006), and is a regular contributor to *Today's Christian Woman*

Leota Jeffrey is a freelance writer who has contributed to *Today's Christian Woman* magazine

Kim Kasch is a freelance writer living in Portland, Oregon

Scott Kays, president and founder of Kays Financial Advisory Corporation, is author of *Achieving Your Financial Potential* (Doubleday, 2000)

Jay Kesler is the preaching pastor of Upland Community Church, in Upland, Indiana. He was president of Youth for Christ from 1973–1985 and president of Taylor University from 1985–2000. He is the author of nearly thirty books, including *Restoring a Loving Marriage* (Cook Communications, 1992)

Jim Killam is co-author of *When God Is the Life of the Party* (NavPress, 2003)

Jane A. G. Kise is an education consultant and freelance writer. She is author of several books, including *Differentiation Through Personality Types* (Corwin Press, 2006)

Diane Mandt Langberg is a licensed psychologist and author of *Counseling Survivors of Sexual Abuse* (Tyndale, 1997) and *On the Threshold of Hope: Opening the Door to Healing for Survivors of Sexual Abuse* (Tyndale, 1999), and is a regular contributor to *Today's Christian Woman*

Annette LaPlaca is a freelance editor and writer. Formerly, she was senior associate editor of Marriage Partnership magazine. She is the author of several books for children, teens, and parents. She and her husband, David, have four children.

Marlene LeFever, manager of ministry relations for David C. Cook Church Ministries, is a speaker, editor of *Teacher Touch*, a quarterly letter of affirmation for Sunday school teachers, and author of several books, including *Learning Styles: Reaching Everyone God Gave You to Teach* (Cook, 2002)

CONTRIBUTORS

Theresa Lode is a home-schooling mom and freelance writer. She is author of *A Parent to Parent Chat on ADHD* (Mother Lode Publishing, 2007)

Maria Lopez is a pseudonym for a writer living in Chicago

Gail MacDonald is author of several books, including *High Call, High Privilege* (Hendrickson Publishers, 2000)

Frederica Mathewes-Green writes regularly for NPR's Morning Edition, Beliefnet.com, *Christianity Today*, and other publications. Her latest book is *Gender: Men, Women, Sex, Feminism* (Conciliar Press, 2002)

Karen L. Maudlin is a licensed clinical psychologist specializing in marriage and family therapy. She is author of *Sticks and Stones* (W Publishing Group, 2002)

Scottie May is professor of Christian formation and ministry at Wheaton (IL) College and an author of *Children Matter: Celebrating Their Place in the Church, Family, and Community* (Wm. B. Eerdmans, 2005)

Melissa and **Louis McBurney** are marriage therapists and co-founders of Marble Retreat in Marble, Colorado. They wrote *Real Questions, Real Answers About Sex* (Zondervan, 2005)

Faith Tibbetts McDonald is a writer and a former teacher

Ginger McFarland Kolbaba is editor of *Marriage Partnership* magazine. Formerly she was associate editor of *Today's Christian Woman*. She is author of *Dazzled to Frazzled and Back Again: The Bride's Survival Guide* (Revell, 2004), and *Surprised by Remarriage: A Guide to the Happily Even After* (Revell, 2006).

Ruth McGinnis is an author, recording artist, and wellness professional. She is the author of *Breathing Freely* (Revell, 2002) and *Living the Good Life* (Baker, 2006), a guide based on her experiences as a personal trainer

Deborah McNaughton, founder of the Financial Victory Institute, has written several books about finances, including *The Get Out Of Debt Kit* (Kaplan Business, 2002), and *Financially Secure: An Easy-To-Follow Money Program For Women* (Thomas Nelson Publishers, 2002)

Holly G. Miller is a travel editor for *The Saturday Evening Post* and teaches journalism at Anderson (Indiana) University. She has written several books, including *Feature and Magazine Writing: Action, Angles, and Anecdotes* (Blackwell, 2005)

Dr. Lana G. Nelson is a surgeon specializing in bariatric surgery at the University of South Florida Health Sciences Center

Carrie Oliver is a marriage and family counselor. Gary J. Oliver is co-author of *A Woman's Forbidden Emotion* (Regal, 2005) and executive director of The Center for Relationship Enrichment at John Brown University

Stormie Omartian, Ruth Senter, and **Colleen Evans** are authors of *Can I Afford Time for Friendships: Answers to Questions Women Ask About Friends* (Bethany House, 1994)

John Ortberg is author of *If You Want to Walk on Water, You've Got to Get Out of the Boat* (Zondervan, 2003) and pastor of Menlo Park Presbyterian Church, in Menlo Park, California

Nancy Ortberg, a church leadership consultant and popular speaker, was formerly a teaching pastor at Willow Creek Community Church in South Barrington, Illinois. She now lives in Menlo Park, California, and is a regular contributor to *Today's Christian Woman*

Leslie Parrott is a marriage and family therapist in Washington. With her husband, Dr. Les Parrott, she co-directs the Center for Relationship Development at Seattle Pacific University. Together they co-authored more than two dozen books, including *Love Talk* (Zondervan, 2004) and *Relationships* (Zondervan, 2002). They speak in more than 40 cities annually, and Leslie is a regular contributor to *Today's Christian Woman*

Mary Ellen Pellegrini is a freelance writer living in Girard, Virginia

Dave Ramsey is host of a nationally syndicated radio show and author of several books, including *The Total Money Makeover* (Thomas Nelson, 2003)

Rhonda Rhea is a speaker, radio personality, mom, and author of several books, including *Amusing Grace* (Life Journey, 2003)

Holly Vicente Robaina has been a professional writer since 1995 and been writing for Christian publications such as *Today's Christian Woman*, since 2002, and is a regular contributor to *Today's Christian Woman*

Douglas Rosenau is a psychologist and marriage and family therapist. He is a nationally known speaker, and author of *A Celebration of Sex* (Thomas Nelson, 2002) and *Slaying the Marriage Dragons* (Victor Books, 1991)

Donna Savage, a freelance writer, lives in Nevada

Marlo M. Schalesky, a freelance writer, lives in California. She is the author of several books, including *Empty Womb, Aching Heart* (Bethany House, 2001)

Barbara Schiller is executive director of Single Parent Family Resources

Deborah Simons, a freelance writer, lives in Virginia

Annette Smith, an author and speaker, lives with her family in Texas

Tim Stafford is a senior writer for *Christianity Today*. He is author of many books including *Knowing the Face of God; As Our Years Increase* (Wipf & Stock Publishers, 2005); *The Student Bible* (with Philip Yancey; Zondervan, 2002); and *Never Mind the Joneses* (Intervarsity Press, 2004). He and his wife, Popie, live in Santa Rosa, California.

Jane Struck is the editor of *Today's Christian Woman*. Formerly, she was editor of *Christian Bookseller* magazine (today *Christian Retailing*), assistant editor of *Christian Life* magazine (the current *Charisma*), merchandising manager of the now-defunct Betty Crocker magazine, *Sphere*, and an active freelancer. She is married (to Rich) and has two adult daughters.

Ramona Cramer Tucker, senior editor for Tyndale House Publishers, is author of several books, including *A Busy Woman's Guide to a Balanced Life* (Tyndale, 1997) and *Little Minds with Big Hearts* (Moody, 1996)

Denise Turner is a business and life success coach as well as a speaker and writer. She lives in Manhattan, New York

Rachelle Vander Schaaf writes frequently on children's health and safety issues. She lives in Pennsylvania with her husband and children

Jody Veenker is a freelance writer who lives in California

Lisa Welchel, author of *Creative Correction* (Tyndale House, 2005) and *So You're Thinking About Homeschooling* (Multnomah, 2005), is the founder of MomTime Get-A-Ways, and is a regular contributor to *Today's Christian Woman*

Rhonda Wilson is a freelance writer who lives with her family in Texas

Jeanne Winters, author of *Inspirational Home: Simple ideas for uplifting décor and craft* (Creative Faith Place, 2005), is the owner of Creative Faith Place, a Christian home, gift, and idea showplace on the Web.

Susan Alexander Yates is the author of ten books and a regular contributor to *Today's Christian Woman* magazine. She speaks nationally and internationally on marriage and family and is often heard on radio, and is a regular contributor to *Today's Christian Woman*

Engage your world with all your Heart, Soul, Strength & Mind!

Today's Christian Woman encourages women like you to love God and engage your world with all your heart, soul, strength and mind!

From cover to cover, *Today's Christian Woman* is brimming with inviting features and compelling stories that bring a biblical perspective to all aspects of your life. Lively articles on relationships, work-life balance and how to develop a deeper understanding of God's word fill every issue.

To receive a **FREE Trial Issue,** go online and order today.

To order, go to:
TodaysChristianWoman.com/RiskFree